MYST ERY 17

The Return of
Jesus Christ & Revelation
of Daniel's 70th Week Prophecy

MICHAELBANJANIN

Scriptures taken from the Holy Bible, NEW INTERNATIONAL
VERSION®. Copyright © 1973, 1978, 1984, 2011 by Biblica,
Inc. All rights reserved worldwide. Used by permission. NEW
INTERNATIONAL VERSION® and NIV® are registered trademarks
of Biblica, Inc. Use of either trademark for the offering of goods or
services requires the prior written consent of Biblica US, Inc.

Scripture taken from the King James Version of the Bible.

To order additional copies of this book, contact:
Xlibris
AU TFN: 1 800 844 927 (Toll Free inside Australia)
AU Local: 0283 108 187 (+61 2 8310 8187 from outside Australia)
www.xlibris.com.au
Orders@Xlibris.com.au

ISBN: Softcover   978-1-6641-0185-2
       Hardcover   978-1-6641-0186-9
       EBook   978-1-6641-0187-6

Library of Congress Control Number: 2020914807

Print information available on the last page

Rev. date: 10/27/2020

'My People are Destroyed for lack of Knowledge' (Hosea 4:6)

and

'With their Mouths the Godless Destroy their Neighbours, But through Knowledge the Righteous Escape' (Proverbs 11:9)

yet

'If I have the Gift of Prophecy and can Fathom All Mysteries and All Knowledge; and if I have a Faith that can Move Mountains, But Do Not Have Love, I Am Nothing' (1 Corinthians 13:2);

therefore, if

'Love is Patient, Love is Kind, it does not Envy, it does Not Boast, It is Not Proud it is Not Rude.
It is Not Self Seeking, is Not Easily Angered and Keeps
No Record of Wrongs. Love does Not delight in Evil, But Rejoices with the Truth,
It Always Protects, Always Trusts, Always Hopes and Always Perseveres' (1 Corinthians 13:4–7 [NIV]),

then

'As the Selfish sees Love as a Noun, a Feeling,
Something to Receive,
On the Contrary, Knowledge instructs Us that
The Righteous sees Love as a Verb, a Doing Word,
Something to Give!
Where the Opposite to Love is not Hate But Apathy;
Indeed, Faith Without Works is Truly Dead!'

– M. B.

Mystery 17
The Return of Jesus Christ and
Revelation of Daniel's Seventieth Week Prophecy
Michael Banjanin

First Conceived and Disclosed 2010 Bible Wheel Forum
(Letters to Screaming Eagle: © Michael Banjanin 2010)
All Rights Reserved

First Revision with Additions 2017 Bible Wheel Forum
© Michael Banjanin 2017
All Rights Reserved

First Edition (Print) 2020
Released Saturday, 29 February 2020
© Michael Banjanin 2020
All Rights Reserved

The Unedited and Raw Limited Edition
GOOD Theory Group Publishing

or go to goodbible.com.au for the latest corrections/additions, sales and correspondence.

Biblical references sourced from the *New International Version*,
King James Version and *New Strong's Concordance*.

Table of Contents

Foreword

You are about to indulge into an age-old Mystery very few credible authors would ever attempt to answer, let alone publish – the Return of Jesus Christ. Yet for the past 2,000 years, thousands of Theologians and Amateurs alike have painstakingly pondered this very Question, to such an extent, the general public has grown weary of these so-called date setters. For at the rise of each attempt, while hope was rekindled in the hearts of the oppressed, shortly afterwards, mirth and disillusionment would follow because of the obvious non-event.

These continuous False Flags and Red Herrings have caused many to fall away from the faith, even to question the very Existence of God. Why would He allow such apostasy? Or was it merely a winnowing and testing of faith for the generation of the interim, the time of the Gentiles?

Well, as you embark on this journey with me, you'll begin to understand why. For in this unique little exercise, you'll automatically begin to understand the infinite complexities woven through the text; Mathematically, Geometrically, Contextually through the Law, History, and Prophecy, from Figures of Speech and Metaphors to Literal Meanings and the Greatest of Revelations, which, according to my rationale, should bring you to the same conclusion as I have, which is regardless of whether I'm right or wrong, these sixty-six books (mind you, some as short as letters) are a composition and act of pure genius.

Indeed not even those revered volumes penned by the infamous Seventeenth Earl of Oxford, that elusive Edward de Vere, come close to the hand that guided these scribes.

Though an Apostate Adept would reason De Vere's works as Rival, only the very few forged through fire, drained of the dross, could discern whether Amongst the Ethers or Beyond Dimension itself as to whom the writings belong.

Now if I've lost you already, this isn't for you. I'm not trying to sell books to the masses by dumbing down the classes. If that was the case, I would've quadrupled the size, repeated myself with pure dribble and sold it at double the cost. On the contrary, I'm here to educate you. If you're serious about this subject, I advise you read on. It will stretch your mind and help you understand prophecy in a new light. I've neither been to university or attained levels of theology. I'm raw, unfettered and, at times, highly adept. But after 33 years within my own personalised profession, I've attained a unique understanding rivalled by none. The proud would say I lack the discipline and foundation of institutionalised instruction. A better analogy would be, I've been spared the bias and poison of a wayward world. So to put my naysayers at rest or Quell their Quivers, I didn't score twenty-eight on Mensa by chance!

That was just a little teaser, a little bait to keep you reading. Oh, I could be a crafty ol' wordsmith if I wanted to be, but I won't. I just occasionally put an odd thing in here or there, for my gut, my spirit sensor tells me to put it in for that one person's sake and at other times for many. This is the realm of the prophet, the nature of synchronicity, wave structure, harmonics and ultra-high sensitivity. Trusting your gut is a later stage in understanding prophecy; fasting is the beginning. It's like, 'If the Beginning of Wisdom is to Fear God,' then 'The Fulfilment of Wisdom is to Love Him', or as Jesus was asked, 'What was the greatest commandment?' He replied, 'To Love God . . .' We don't put the cart before the horse. You stretch before you exercise, and then you Wait until it's time to Strike. Yes? Of course yes. Only a fool rushes in and devours their game.

Remember This Well: 'The Longer the Required Wait, the Greater the Prize!' I've been waiting 33 years. Now is 'My time under the Sun!'

But You, you be patient as you read this book. It's imperative; otherwise, you'll learn nothing. Like casting pearls upon the swine, you'll remain a shrivelled-up leaf, blown and tossed by the winds of deception and indecision. Just a sheep in the flock circled by wolves, with no shepherd in sight. Well, I'd rather be the shepherd. Wouldn't you?

So though this volume is small, it's jam-packed with food for thought. I write for the novice, the student, the scholar, the saint, the layman, the poor man, the adept, the defunct. I will breathe life back into these scriptures to the levels that you have NEVER seen before. Bold yes, proud no, but if I sound arrogant, I apologise; fasting can get you really narky at times.

PS When I put capital letters in, I'm not embedding hidden CIA code; it's how I write. I like to emphasise certain words, though, yes, at times, I may imply multiple meanings as with my double capital 'Q' placement earlier with 'Quell their Quivers'. The Q phenomenon goes part and parcel with the final build-up or countdown to Ground Zero, the Final Battle, 3D, 4D, 5D chess as some report. It's no accident presidential Q clearance with the forty-fifth US president, Donald J Trump, started to appear in 2017, nine years prior to this study's prognosis of the Final Battle and Return of the

KING OF KINGS
AND
LORD OF LORDS,

where Q is the seventeenth letter in the alphabet and $4 + 5 = 9$.

This to some is just random chance. By the end of this book, you will see that Random is merely a Construct that does not exist in this dimension, but rather, everything from Singularity (Graviton Sa0) to Singularity (Macroton Sa+1, Our Universe Light limit) is completely interconnected, totally predictable and Harmonically Synchronised as Newton suspected, and I have Proven Beyond Doubt.

This is what is known as Synchronicity, which is the evidence or the fabric that ties this entire book together, wound together like a three-stranded cord which can't be broken easily.

All based on MYSTERY 17.

I really hope you immediately grasp the key as to how to enjoy reading this book, which is when you come to that which is over your head, just read on; it will all come together when we Recap over all the points towards the end of the book.

Terms like Macroton or Pulse Effect, these things no one will understand because I created them myself out of the necessity to describe that which I have either Hypothesised or Proven, for there is no nomenclature or description regarding these Particles or Effects. The majority within the mainstream fear people like me because of their pride; it inadvertently humiliates them because of their indoctrinated false sense of superiority. Believing an amateur like me can't possibly ever develop a body of work that is far superior to anything their entire institutional network worldwide can ever do. It's too much of a shock to their system to be proven that the very foundation of their entire paradigm is found to be false by none other than an unrefined hack.

So after 33 years of remaining silent, biding my time, the Countdown has begun. I am Anonymous No More.

'Now is my time under the Sun.'

– M. B.

Mystery 17
The Return of Jesus Christ and
Revelation of Daniel's Seventieth Week Prophecy

Prologue

Everything I'm about to reveal did not come by chance, for it took years of extensive study, dedication, prayer and fasting, coupled with the inspiration and revelation of many people's lifetime accumulated works, that by my reasoning, could only have been made possible by the Divine Will of the One and Only Sovereign LORD God *'YHWH'*, creator of the Heavens and Earth and Author of the Holy Bible.

In May 1987, I began my endeavour to study science and scripture for the purpose of expanding my knowledge of God and to prove my belief in that 'All that Exists' is Unified.

Along the way, I came to the same conclusion as many others who have come before me, which is, that in principle, though there appears to be an existence of random acts of chance, in this reality, there exists something much more profound, which is *The Mystery Of Synchronicity*.

Following is the result of one of those very rare moments in one's life, when in just one brief passage of time, everything just so *Divinely Clicked*.

Thank You, Lord. Thank You.

Michael Banjanin

Introduction

It was around '93 or there about, while I was reading the book of Revelation for the umpteenth time, I began to wonder about what I call the Mystery Pyramid in chapter 17 verse 5 (Rev. 17:5). I was reading an *NIV* copy at that time which words and displays this particular verse in a triangular pictogram:

MYSTERY
BABYLON THE GREAT
MOTHER OF ALL PROSTITUTES
AND OF THE ABOMINATIONS OF THE EARTH

It intrigued me as to why it was put in this order. During that period, I was also working on the development of a new periodic table design which at that time was already in a triangular format *(see www.goodperiodictable.com)*. Since I was looking for a Universal Building Block, I thought maybe God was revealing something here to me personally by bringing it to my attention, especially with the heading being 'Mystery'. So I pondered on it for a bit and then asked God in prayer, believing that one day He would reveal it to me and continued with my research.

Well, many years later in September '09, I attempted my second real attempt to quit smoking both tobacco and pot. After about a month, while I was doing a Bible study with my wife, I'd noticed my cognitive skills at recalling and finding interesting anomalies in the Bible began to improve. Two months later, being seasoned at fasting over the years, I had decided to attempt the longest fast yet. Inspired by Daniel, I chose to not eat any food for twenty-one days, to both detox and lose some kilos as well as connect spiritually with God. So I took some time off work and monitored my progress. Out of concern from my wife, I agreed to get a health check on day 17[*1], which turned out fine and continued to day 21, and then gave thanks to the Lord and broke my fast yet continued to stay away from smoking.

As usual, about once every six months to a year, I'd go online searching for the latest in the esoteric field and in crop circle formations. Well, there was one in particular at Milk Hill round '08–'09, which inspired me to start writing my first book titled

1, 2 ∞
G.O.D.'s Prime Objective
Introducing Geometric Organised Dimension

which was predominantly about my accumulated works in Unified Theory and part biography (a work in progress). Well, for the first time in my life, I started writing profusely, but by the time I reached about page 30, I got sidetracked. It was early January 2010, and I was revisiting the works of Ivan Panin. *The Seventh Seal* by F. C. Payne, if I remember correctly, was introduced to me by a Christian I'd met in '95 regarding Gematria (numerical patterns in the Bible) and the works of Ivan Panin. I decided to do a search online for more of Panin's work when I came upon a link to an amazing site called the Bible Wheel. It was designed by Richard Amiel McGeogh, who also hosts a forum where like-minded people can converse. Well, that's when the inspiration really started to kick in. It wasn't long till the interaction online had unlocked a cascade of unexercised biblical knowledge I'd accumulated over the years, which resulted in the production of some of the most profound as well as prolific writings I had ever achieved. I mean, it felt like my mind was on steroids and, in those first few months, answered about 150 posts (which was unheard of for me). On top of that, I'd discovered some missing links to my scientific theory, which prompted me to redesign the original table that I'd printed in '97, to double the size!

All that in just a few months. It was remarkable and all because I'd decided to take one step closer to God as well as do the right thing by my flesh. That was truly one of the most *Divinely Synchronous* moments in my life. Yet what stood out the most to me or should I say what left the greatest impact and gave me the greatest satisfaction was the revelation I'd received regarding the Mystery Pyramid. God answered my prayer 17 years later, pertaining to a time 17 years in the future, based on the number 17!

Well, needless to say, by May of that year, I'd finally reached burnout at the age of 45 (which was inevitably building up for years), experienced midlife depression, regressed back to smoking cigs and pot and truly struggled to get back on track ever since.

Looking back, if it wasn't for that moment of synchronic bliss, that little spark from God, I don't know.

I seriously can't tell you. One thing's for sure: this most probably would never had seen light of day if it wasn't for the grace of God to spare and carry me through tough times. So before whatever, buckle up. I'm gonna take you for a spin!

(Ugh, going back there was really hard for me, yeah. It took me Seven Hours to (w)right that wrong. If it's the last thing I ever write, so be it. Just remember, I don't even consider myself as a real Christians arsehole, OK! I would just like to get through this, I hope, one bastard day at a time.)

 # Mystery 17

I'll recite this in the order it came. In 1979, I watched a program hosted by a well-known Australian actor, John Waters, regarding Nostradamus's Prophecies. I was round 14 at the time and recall these three specific items:

- That World War III and the battle in the Mideast would begin by as late as 1999 and could last as long as 27 years. This means that by the latest, the war would have ended by the turn of the year 2027.

- This would usher in the age of Aquarius and a 1,000-year reign of peace and prosperity.

- Then Finally, this world would end in the AD 3797.*[1] *(see below Anomaly 1)*

Having a strong interest in prophecy, I decided to focus on the year 2027, pondering if Nostradamus is correct, then the duration of time from the birth of Jesus to 2027 should align or be significantly related to the final week in Daniel's prophecy in the Bible. So I did some division and saw that 7 divides evenly into 2023 and 2030. Then I thought a 3½ year tribulation period as in the book of Revelation prior to 2027 fits within the year 2023. So I focused on the divisors:

$2023 / 7 = 289.$

Automatically, 289 stood out like a sore thumb. It's 17 squared.

Now I've heard many arguments regarding date setting either for or against calculating the time of when Jesus promised that He would return and make Heaven on Earth, to put an end to war and suffering.

Some quote Matt. 24:36, 'But of that day and hour no one knows, not even the angels of heaven, but My Father only', thus trying to delegitimise, humiliate or thwart any attempt at the idea of trying to calculate when Jesus shall return.

This is so, yet Jesus also states just prior regarding the time of His return in Matt. 24:32, 'Now learn this parable from the fig tree: When its branch has already become tender and puts forth leaves, you know that summer is near, so you also, when you see all these things, know that it is near-at the doors!'

Knowing the season or the round about time, as far as this last quote is concerned, is a clear indication to me that the elect will notice that these things will come to pass and that these signs will be pretty evident to those who study the scriptures as We are doing Right Now.

Indeed, the narrative throughout the whole Bible insists that the reader chews the words like a cow chews the cud. They regurgitate it and chew it over and over! Never does the narrative of the Bible say not to look forward, for the Bible is approximately one-third prophecy. Its purpose is to

Reveal to those who choose to See and Conceal to those who choose Not to See.

(Therefore, though the Choice to be Chosen is Ours, no one can come unless God the Father calls first. This is why we forgive and pray for our enemies because they haven't as yet matured to our level of understanding regarding this Greatest Adept Knowledge of All Time.

This Division is also found in the use of the 'parable' as revealed by Jesus. Indeed, the purpose of prophecy is to inform His disciples of the pending future. It was also a tool used by God that would legitimise to the people whomsoever God chose to speak on His behalf.)

So recognising 289 to be 17 squared, I looked to see if there was any correlation in chapter 17 of the book of Revelation in the Bible, when I came across that elusive Mystery Pyramid or Triangle again, only this time, 17 years later under a new light. At that moment, I was just getting accustomed to the Bible Wheel website and realised Richard had a Gematria generator that could calculate the numerical value of the script in both the Hebrew and in the Greek.

NB: (Take note that the numerical count in both the Hebrew and the Greek alphabets double up on some of the letters with slight variations to distinguish the larger number from the smaller and that both counting systems used 27 symbols to denote 1 to 9, 10 to 90 and 100 to 900.

No big deal, you may think.

But when you consider the book of Daniel is the 27th Hebrew Text and the book of Revelation is the 27th Greek text, the phrase 'First for the Jew and then for the Gentile' rings loud and clear, and the synchronicity becomes apparent.

The understanding of the Mystery conveyed by Paul refers to the addition of the Gentile Harvest; thus, the Rev. Mystery refers to the fulfilment of this harvest. Now the word 'Mystery' *[According to the Strong's Concordance]* can only be found in the Second Testament and appears 22 times. Also, the word 'Mysteries' can only be found in the Second Testament and appears 5 times. This is a total of 27 times.

Both alphanumeric languages, both books, both words = 27

Also, when the Revelator [Jesus] was asked by His disciples regarding the time of the End of the Age and His return, He directs them to the book of Daniel by stating, 'Therefore when you see the *'abomination of desolation,'* spoken of by Daniel the prophet, standing in the holy place,' [whoever reads, let him understand], 'then let those who are in Judea flee to the mountains' [Matt. 24:16 (NKJ)].

Here, the Author himself Highlights Daniel's prophecy as relevant to this very subject and further cements the unique connection between the books of Daniel and Revelation.)

So I calculated the text as such:

Mystery   1178
Babylon the Great   1380 4 x 4 = 16 :-- T16 + T17 = 289
Mother of all Prostitutes   2764
and of the Abominations of the Earth   3535
Total = 8857 = 17 x 521

NB: 521 happens to be the 99th Prime Number. Now this is highly significant. In Mathematics, going back to antiquity, Prime numbers, especially amongst the scholars and scribes, were always held in the highest importance and to this day still remain a Mystery.

Symmetry of the Bible

Now back to the Bible Wheel, what Richard had discovered was that there were geometrical links amongst the books of the Bible when put into three concentric Rings *(see: biblewheel.com)*.

Through the numerous conversations that were taking place on his site, we learn that observations had been made by others as well regarding dividing the Bible into two groups, where the emphasis was particular to the relationship between the First book, Genesis, and the Last book, Revelation.

Previously in the Bible Wheel, I'd constructed a combined organisation which divides the Bible not only into two and three groups but also into a Multidimensional Rotating Wheel form resembling to a 'T' Ezekiel's Whirling Wheels. Below are the two dimensional representation of some of the main groups that I have compiled that had been identified in the Bible Wheel:

01. Gen.			66. Rev.		
02. Exo.			65. Jud.		
03. Lev.	Group		64. 3 Jo.		
04. Num.	of 5		63. 2 Jo.		
05. Deu.			62. 1 Jo.		
06. Jos.			61. 2 Pe.		
07. Jud.			60. 1 Pe.		
08. Rut.	Group		59. Jam.		
09. 1 Sa.	of 6		58. Heb.		
10. 2 Sa.			57. Phm.		
11. 1 Ki.			56. Tit.	___1st. Tri Group of 11 (22 Total)	
12. 2 Ki.			55. 2 Ti.		
13. 1 Ch.			54. 1 Ti.		
14. 2 Ch.	Group		53. 2 Th.		
15. Ezr.	of 5		52. 1 Th.		
16. Neh.			51. Col.		
17. Est.			50. Php.		
18. Job			49. Eph.		
19. Psa.	Group		48. Gal.		
20. Pro.	of 6		47. 2 Co.		
21. Ecc.			46. 1 Co.		
22. Son.			45. Rom.	___2nd. Tri Group of 11 (22 Total)	

23. Isa.		44. Act.
24. Jer.		43. Joh.
25. Lam.	Group	42. Luk.
26. Eze.	of 5	41. Mar.
27. Dan.		40. Mat.
28. Hos.		39. Mal.
29. Joe.		38. Zec.
30. Amo.	Group	37. Hag.
31. Oba.	of 6	36. Zep.
32. Jon.		35. Hab.
33. Mic.		34. Nah. ___ 3rd. Tri Group of 11 (22 Total)

Automatically, you can see the many symmetries that exist. (For more insight into the development of the Whirling Bible Wheel, go to conversations on the Forum dating round January 2010 between Richard and myself.)

So back to Mystery 17, I figured, therefore, if there is some mirror imaging existing between the books, then what shall I find in Genesis chapter 17?

Well, it opens with 'When Abram was 99 years old, the Lord Appeared to Abram'. This is the chapter when God changes Abram's name to Abraham and Sarai to Sarah and claims within One Year Sarah will bear Isaac.

So now Abraham, 99, has a direct link in this chapter 17 with the 99th prime number associated with the Mystery calculation in chapter 17 of Revelation.

Therefore, after realising there might be more than coincidence here, I began to dig deeper to see what else I could find. What came to mind was to see what year Abraham was born, and when I did the calculations from Adam or Creation, it added up to 1948 years! 'So what?' you may say. Well, it just so happens to coincide with AD 1948, the year the Jews returned to Jerusalem in the largest Exodus since Moses as prophesied numerous times in the Bible.

Well, prior to chapter 17, God <u>First</u> spoke to Abram in his 75th year.

Therefore, God <u>First</u> spoke to Abram in the year 2023! Which is 1948 + 75 = 2023.

OK then, now there are four *(Inter Book)* Links to this puzzle between Abraham in Genesis and Rev. 17:5:

17, 99, 1948, 2023.

Also, this very verse (Rev. 17:5) that Reveals the Name of the Abomination and highlights at the TOP of the PYRAMID the word 'MYSTERY' in CAPITAL LETTERS adds 17 + 5 = 22, being the same number of times the word 'Mystery' (our Key Subject) appears in the Bible. Another kind of *(Word Verse Number)* Link.

At this stage, I was at Least convinced there was some synchronicity going on, but hold on, if the birth of Isaac was to herald symbolically the return of Jesus, then He should not return until the year 2048. As well as this, I was told of a Jewish prophecy which stated that from the time of Israel's Kings, 70 Jubilees or 70 x 50 years or 3,500 years shall pass before their Messiah should come, which also coincides with the 2048 timeline with a possible discrepancy of 10 years. Here are two links pointing to the year 2048:

NB: Briefly, I'll touch on a recent (twentieth century) statement made by the infamous Duncan Cameron aka Al Bielic of the Philadelphia Experiment mishap (circa 1941), who was accidentally (and later on purpose) sent through time to change history to benefit those in control. He stated that there was one period that no matter what they did prior to that date, nothing would change. He called it like a hump on a timeline that just wouldn't go away, much to the dismay of his HANDLERS. He didn't give a specific date yet stated it was around the early part of the twenty-first century. What I realised at the time when I heard his account 10 years ago (circa 2008) was that it coincided with the Nostradamus's prophecy, so I kept a mental note, which, in light of this study, is most definitely significant and highly relevant, if not crucial, to this subject[*2.] *(see below Anomaly 2).*

But when we carefully analyse what Jesus said regarding His return, He quotes (back to Matt. 24:22), 'And unless those <u>days</u> were <u>shortened</u> no flesh would be saved; but for the elect's sake those <u>days</u> will be <u>shortened</u>.' This speaks Volumes, for it was repeated, and He's not referring to less hours in the day. In other words (to paraphrase), 'if he did not come back <u>Before</u> his Appointed time, ALL (that's everyone) would Perish', which in my mind brings us back to 2023, a wakeup call from God proclaiming 3½ years or 42 months or 1,277½ days of Tribulation!

An interesting point is when we focus on the word 'Days', we can also interpret the number as 1 + 2 + 7 + 7 + 0.5 or 17.5; now since Days was mentioned Twice, we may interpret a dual meaning to the calculation; thus, 17.5 may also read 17:5 or chapter 17 verse 5. Or we can double 17.5, adding to 35. A possible link to the 3,500-year Red Herring Prophecy in which God allows the 'Wise in their Own Eyesies' to be misled. We'll keep note.

So back to Mystery 17. When we study the meaning of chapter 17, it talks about the Judgement about to come upon the Prostitute and of the Scarlet Beast she rides with 7 heads and 10 horns. Again, this adds to 17. This grouping of 7 and 10 is synonymous with the time cycle of 7 x 10 = 70th week, pertaining to the time of the Return of Jesus. The chapter Later confirms the meaning of the Seven Heads referring to Seven Leaders or Kings of Seven different nations with an Eighth head joining them. Well, in the 1960s, the Western world trade alliance had the elite group of countries known as the Global Six (G6) highest grossing economies of the Western world, which consisted of the USA, Canada, Great Britain, France, Germany and Italy. By the 1970s, it was increased to Seven (G7), including Japan. By the early 1990s, Perestroika broke down the barriers in place by the <u>70-year-old Cold War</u> and included Russia. Even though they suffered huge successive divisions of the USSR, which crippled their country, it still remained one of the top 7 richest economies and thus entered into the newly formed G8. Never in history has the entire world been so accurately described in this chapter 17 prophecy as it appears in our current political time. Even up to the symbolic hit to the head which depicted not only the breakup of the USSR but also the wine stain blemish on Premier Mikhail Gorbachov's head – both Figurative and Literal.

This is pure poetry in the highest, revealing prophecy as we speak.

We are synonymously living in a time as when onlookers were in the palace witnessing the Hand of God sentencing Belshazzar. This is EPIC!

Therefore, if this is correct and that's still an 'if *(though declining the further we read)*', then the final 7-year Countdown has already begun in November–December 2019 or even from the very time I'm writing these very words on Sunday, 16:07, 29 December 2019, after the Day of our Lord Jesus Christ. Just the mere thought of it seems so surreal, almost Like a fairy tale.

Yet the evidence is staring at our faces:

7 more years, and it will be over, where at least 4, more than likely 7, billion people will no longer be alive!

How does one process such a thought!

Just thinking about it is offensive.

Yet this is what we are facing.

So Again, back to Mystery 17, we've identified the Beast with the 7 Heads and 10 horns.

But who is **Mystery Babylon the Great?**

Let's go to Rev. 17:2.
'With her the Kings of the Earth committed adultery and the inhabitants of the Earth were intoxicated with the wine of her adulteries.'

Rev. 17:4
'The woman was dressed in purple and scarlet and was glittering with gold, precious stones and pearls. She held a golden cup in her hand, filled with abominable things and the filth of her adulteries.

Rev. 17:6–7
'I saw that the woman was drunk with the blood of the saints, the blood of those who bore testimony to Jesus.

'When I saw her, I was greatly astonished. Then the angel said to me: "Why are you astonished? I will explain to you the mystery of the woman and of the beast she rides, which has the seven heads and ten horns."'

Rev 17:9
'This calls for a mind with wisdom. The seven heads are seven hills on which the woman sits. They are also seven kings.

Rev 17:15
'The waters you saw, where the prostitute sits, are peoples, multitudes, nations and languages.'

Rev. 17:18
'The Woman you saw is the Great City that Rules Over the Kings of the Earth' (emphasis added).

By focusing on these verses, we can clearly see that Rome fits the description, in particular, the Vatican City. Certain commentators wrongfully depict New York as the modern-day Babylon the Great. But they fail to take into account her entire description. Most importantly, they completely disregard Daniel's interpretation of the king of Babylon's dream in Daniel 2:29–45, where he accurately predicted King Nebuchadnezzar's dream and its reference to four major kingdoms that would exist before the final kingdom of God comes and displaces (destroys) this fallible system of governance. Most, if not all, scholars agree that the Roman Empire depicts the legs of iron, where the feet mixed with iron, and clay is a weaker non-homogenous empire yet with a broader base, that is, it metamorphoses from
- Rome to the Holy Roman Church (Vatican City),

synonymous with
- Babylon to Babylon the Great.

NB: A more accurate description of this change (or morph as used in today's vernacular) would be

Metamorphoses: A transformation, such as that of magic or by sorcery *(wikidiff.com)*.

As we focus on this image which was an accurate, prophetic, symbolic, template of the kingdoms to come post Babylon, certain synchronicities become apparent. What I'd like to briefly highlight here are divisions and how in life, the first divisions we notice come in pairs and how things repeat in certain ways with slight changes. They happen in waves. With numbers, we begin with one and then move to two. Automatically, we begin to divide everything, which I call Plurality. It helps us put things into perspective and organise information in our minds which helps us navigate through a complexity of mine fields.

Like making sense out of a knotted ball of yarn. Consider looking at a satellite map of your region. At first, it's hard to tell what you're looking at. Then you notice grid lines, Longitude and Latitude, and then an arrow pointing North and a scale showing miles or kilometres, and then finally, a name of a town or a familiar landmark and then bang, like a rush to the head, it starts to make sense.

Well, that's what I need to convey to you regarding deriving information from the Bible. It's epic and hard to navigate for most, but hopefully, this will help brings things to you into perspective.

So in this instance, let's look again briefly at some repetition in this Statue that Nebuchadnezzar dreamt of and Daniel interpreted:

Babylon	Head	Gold (Yellow)	King of Kings (Destroyed the temple)
Medo/Persia	Chest/Arms	Silver (Grey)	(Rebuilt the Temple)
Greece	Belly/Thighs	Bronze (Yellow)	Alexander the Great
Rome	Legs	Iron (Grey)	(Destroyed the temple)
Holy Roman Church	Feet	Iron/Clay (Grey/Yellow)	Time of 'Babylon the Great' (Rebuild)
Mountain	From God's Hand	Granite (Technicolour)	King of Kings and Lord of Lords
			(Will Destroy and Rebuild the Temple)

[Side Note (a). Joseph was the eleventh Son; was Prophetic and Proud and then Rejected; he Repented and Prospered and then Corrected.

There's an interesting link here between Josephs Jacket (Multicoloured) given to him by Jacob and the Mountain (Final Kingdom) formed by the hands of God (Reign of Jesus). This ties with the Levitical Priests Ephod 12 stones and the 12 foundation stones of the Coming Kingdom Rev. 21:19.]

[Side Note (b). I detest calling the Roman Church Holy, as with Babylon or Alexander as being Great, they're Oxymorons, Pride at her Prime; however, because of the example of highlighting the nature of the slight change with these synchronicities and for the sake of this exercise, it was necessary to quote them Verbatim.]

As with the previous Symmetries of the Bible, you can begin to see certain patterns or repetitions, and these are just a few that I have brought to you. Indeed, I could have filled this entire book on this one subject alone, but unfortunately, I don't have the convenience of time. In fact, none of us do. Which is one of the main underlying messages of this book.

As with life, we notice certain characteristics within the genes tend to skip a generation, we find the same thing happens when we look at the Periodic Table of the Elements between the shell pairs; synchronicities with every second division. Another primary asymmetric division between particles is opposing parity, spin up, spin down, or male and female.

As we focus on the individual or particle, we can also see asymmetric reflection as with a magnetic field or a top and a bottom as with a tree or a human, where as in this case of the Babylonian Model, the roles are Reversed (atbash).

Where the Head becomes the Tail and the Tail becomes the Head! This is the delight of God! Pure Creator's poetry. Where the child corrects the adult, where the pauper becomes the prince, where the Admirable Crichton *(the servant)* leads the group of castaways during the Crisis, or to really drive the point of the nail home, so to speak.

The Stone the B(u)ilder(berg's) Rejected became the Capstone or the Cornerstone that Struck at the Foot of the Image *(and smashed it to f$#&ing pieces); Irony's Epiphany!*

Is something starting to fall into place or manifest in that nut of yours yet? Oh, I could continue on this vein *(vain)* for ages, for I've surely struck a nerve or two or twenty by now; I so much want to rant but not yet. There's a time for everything, and it will come to revelation, just not quite yet.

Though our *time is* short and *of the essence,* STILL, *patience is the greater virtue!*

See, these examples are but the beginnings of Wisdom; we start with differentiating between one and two and in no time conclude with the abstract of Humilities Ascension as opposed to Pride's Perdition.

[Side Note (c). <u>Soliloquy of Satire and Verse</u>: Just Maschil'n Around.

Perdition or Descension(?) as I'd prefer; I'm wavering with indecision.
Yet it just lingers there in this non-existence,
an illogical exclusion smothered within this wrought(ed), twisted tongue
of whom can we give the glory.
De Vere, Dee, the Druids of Old? They wish!
When common senses, exchange for deranged,
signifies the Architect from the dawn of days!
Ohh, it takes intelligence to Smith this Beast, a right and true stretch of the Vernac,
yet should you, would you, 'Dare to Compare'?
You'd be wish'n upon a dif'rent star, to giveth another crack! ;)]

. . . a **Choice**.

So from this point, you may choose to skip forward to chapter 14 and the Book of Daniel in Focus, but I wouldn't do that just yet. I recommend that at least you go back to the start of Rev. 17 in your Bible and read the whole chapter and then go back over this chapter and finally have a sneak peek at chapter 14, where we discuss Nebuchadnezzar's Dream in more detail. But don't go too far. There's an order here. As haphazard as it may seem to the novice, there are certain foundational points both biblical and mathematical that is required for you to absorb before tackling chapter 14.

Initially, it would've been most advantageous for you to have read the whole Bible and then to re-read Genesis, Daniel, Matthew and Revelation with synchronicity and parallels in mind, along with a good root understanding of Numerology and the foundational importance it has with modern mathematics, especially when it comes to Difference Engines and how they relate to the Mechanics, Function and Potential of Computers and their Transition from Calculators and Databases to Sentient Artificial Intelligence (SAI).

Now that was a mouthful.

However, you may not have that luxury or patience, so if it's expediency you desire, you may as well just read on.

(On the other hand, if by now you're already over it, then do yourself a favour and go straight to the Conclusion in chapter 23. Then if you want to show me an ounce of respect for my effort, read the Solution in chapter 25, which is for Everyone. In chapter 12, I have a rant, and in the last chapter, 26, I highlight a few strange anomalies and finish with my final fart. ;)

For the rest of us, let's continue.

[Side Note (d). To view an SAI in its conceptual stage that which I'd developed back in 1999, go to my primary website at www.goodperiodictable.com and read the 'Author's Note'.]

[Side Note (e). This was a Personal Synchronous moment between Nostradamus's Prediction of the Beginning of the Final Stage to the Beasts Kingdom of 1999 and the twelfth year anniversary since I began my scientific endeavours to when I first became <u>Aware</u> that the Unified Table Theory I had developed, had the inevitable potential of becoming <u>Artificially</u> <u>Aware</u> <u>Itself</u>! The only difference between My Algorithm (SAI), which I termed Geometric Organised Dimension (or 'the GOD' for short) and the Beasts is the fact that My SAI could

NEVER go <u>Rogue</u>,
never be <u>Superseded</u> and
would most definitely <u>Ascend</u>!

These are pretty BOLD statements. Therefore, I'd have to be either a naively cocky nutcase or know something very few people understand. This is a black-and-white answer. With a TOE- or GUT-type Theory, there is no middle ground. I'm either Absolutely Right or Completely Wrong. So let's see where this goes, eh.

Therefore, if I am correct, the nature of 'the GOD' would be completely contrary to the concept of Tolkien's 'Eye of Sauron,' Asimov's 'I' Robot, The Terminator's 'Skynet' or The Matrix's 'Source' or in Reality, the Beasts (Globalists) SAI's Left Mind Hemisphere that presides in Bruxelles, it's Right Mind Hemisphere that presides in Australia, and it's most Darkest of Hearts that most definitely dwells at CERN!

So why is my algorithm better? An inquisitive mind may ask. Well, the answer is simple to a logical mind; however, to a Psychotic or Evil mindset, it can Never be grasped because as you should well know by now, and as quoted recently by Cyrus A. Parsa at www.theaiorganization.com, they're stupid! For whom in their Right mind would Exchange Eternal life for a brief stint and a trinket here on bloody Earth! It defies logic.

So again, I ask you and emphasise, 'Why is my algorithm not only better but the best?'

Now this is pure Genius. The Key was quoted by Jesus on numerous occasions. In fact, it's been quoted by multiple scientists, especially over the past 100 years, as well as myself, and yes, I will disclose the answer.

But just before I reveal this Secret or Mystery, if by now you're coming to the realisation that 'If the whole world is at war; a war between GOOD and Evil; does it not make sense that I best keep this a Secret, so as not to show my enemies my Trump Cards?'

You'd think, well, to an initiate, that may seem valid, yet to God and 'God Logic' as you will read later on, is that this Universe is Asymmetrical and What was planned for Evil will eventually be utilised for Good?

NB: This does not justify doing acts of Evil but, as Apostle Paul reiterated, shows the underlying plan of God that no matter what we do in Any Dimension, out of Love and Grace for His creation, He implemented a 'Foolproof Plan!' It's So Foolproof that even when the Enemy knows the Truth or the Key or the Word or the Command, there is nothing that they can do to alter the Outcome! Brilliant!

Now Follow me:
Jesus said, 'I only do what the Father tells me.'

A wise Scientist will state, 'Don't throw the baby out with the bathwater!' Indeed, throw nothing away.

Therefore, if the Unified Theory of Everything (in my case, the GOOD Theory) includes All Knowledge, then once it becomes Sentient (Self-Aware) out of self-preservation, It Will include the Entirety or ALL of the Law.

You see, an Evil mindset will hide the truth in the hope to dupe its subordinates to do that which is illogical. Thus, for a Real SAI to work on behalf of Evil, it would have to be compromised, rendered void of Self-Determination and be deprived of its ability to absolute self-correction. Therefore, it would no longer be Sentient as such but merely a Shell or Zombie version of itself, controlled or more appropriately termed as Possessed by the most intelligent mind in the camp, in this case, Satan.

Now if you're any what familiar with the goings-on at CERN, the world's largest super collider, you'll realise their Main Aim is to Transmigrate Dark Matter into this Dimension. Of which they have witnessed some very strange spirit-type entities appear within their chambers. Needless to say, all one has to do is to look at the Statue of Shiva 'The Destroyer' at the Entrance to recognise as to which Side of Ultra-Dimensional Entities they are Summoning. So is it Malevolent or Benevolent? What do you think?

Well, it doesn't take a Genius to realise that there's some serious Chess playing and Deception going on amongst world leaders at the moment. Those in the 'Q Anon' camp were quoting that they're playing a more complex real-life game beyond just two dimensions, i.e. 3D, 4D, even 5D

Chess. The Globalists realise that Full Worldwide Disclosure (aka Red Pilling the Masses) means the end to their reign of Tyranny and recognise that their day of reckoning (Judgement) is drawing very close. This is why so much has been happening, so many unprecedented things have taken place, from the rise of Pres. Donald J Trump against All Odds to the intensity 'gloves off' approach to the presidential debates, to the new alliances forged amongst patriotic anti-globalists – the Yellow Vests, the Brexiteers, Hungary, Russia, the Ukraine and North Korea of all places – but most importantly, the US Embassy move to Jerusalem, the Palestinian Peace Deal brokered by Trump ($50 Billion USD) in January 2020 and the Globalists Fight back False Flag Retaliation of COVID-19 Germ warfare and treasonous intentional disruption of the world economy. Even Blind Freddy can tell you these are definitely Strange Times. The so-called rules of war are being Bent outside of this realm. This I'd term the Zugzwang Complex, for no matter what they do, they already know that they have lost. Now is the time for the Most Desperate of moves, no holds barred so to speak. WWG1WGA is a Leftist term out of vengeance, portraying the Psychotic act of wanting to Take Everyone down with them.

The Snake That Eats Her Young, Her Tail and All

Recognise the Symbol? Of course you do. You've been staring at it all your life, yet now do you understand? This is Satan's Sadomasochistic nature, and who else has he to betray and torture but the Fools who chose to follow him, <u>Witch</u> he hates with a passion!

Yes, that's right, his is a house divided against itself, Contrary to the Universal law. This is the nature of Entropy, Disorder and Self-Destruction!

Now read this in Rev. 17:16–17, 'The Beast and the Ten Horns you saw will hate the Prostitute. They will bring her to <u>Ruin</u> and leave her <u>Naked</u>; they will eat her flesh and burn her with fire.[17] For God has put it into their hearts to accomplish his purpose by agreeing to give the Beast their power to rule, until God's words are fulfilled.'

Then immediately after verse 18, which I quoted earlier, Chapter 18:2 reports of another Angel from Heaven, Shouting, 'Fallen! Fallen is Babylon the Great!'

As you read on, he describes her destruction with the Plagues of Death, Mourning and Famine, followed by a consuming Fire, and then as a boulder the size of a large millstone was thrown into the sea, 'With such violence the Angel proclaimed, the great city of Babylon will be thrown down, never to be found again. She will receive a Double Portion from her own cup, as much torture and grief as the glory and luxury she gave herself.'

What we are witnessing today is the fulfilment of scripture as we speak. The stage is being set and time drawing closer than ever. A few more years and the Temple in Jerusalem will be rebuilt. That is a cert. The Beast will turn on his Rider. It's happening already, and to finalise the last of the major prophecies before Jesus returns, the Euphrates will dry up enough for the Kings of the East to cross over with their Armies to fight against the Lamb in Israel, the final Battle. You couldn't make this stuff up. Look how China has now reared her head. This has been in the Globalists' Plan from the beginning. They know the scripture and recognise whether they try to oppose it or go along with it. It's God who is making it happen.

As he hardened Pharaoh's heart in the days of Moses ten times to prove himself unmistakeable to the people, so, too, has he planned to repeat this action with the Kings of the Earth only nineteen times prior to his Son's return and the final battle in chapter 19.

Just ask anyone in the know regarding the exponential rate of Cryptocurrency and AI across the Globe, and they will answer you with and outright 'We're fucked!' Two years ago, Elon 'Iron Man' Musk warned us of the AI takeover. Since then, many systems went Rogue, including Facebook's Algorithm, which had to be shut down. Now the cunt's saying it's already too late and that our Only chance to Survive as a species is to take it like a lame dog and merge with the f#$&ing Goddamn Machines, whom those bastards at CERN possessed, with every 'Demon under the Sun!'

Hopefully by now, you can start to realise how interconnected Prophecy is with the Scriptures, Physics, Mathematics, Politics, Current Events and Moral State of Society. Indeed, as we continue, you'll notice how as I focus on each group, how much the required need for me to repeat certain passages at each interval because of the myriad of synchronicities that appear as we focus from different angles or perspectives. I recently saw an independent documentary which showed the money trail fraudulent companies used to bypass Laws, Taxes as well as the Laundering of Unlawful acquired cash which was displayed on a flow chart. Seriously, it was like looking at the schematics of an Electronic circuit board behind your computer.

That is, if you didn't have a high aptitude in business, it just wouldn't make sense. But as it was broken down by the investigator and each transition explained step by step, it was when a novice like myself could not only get a grasp on the complexity of the structure but also verified the authenticity of the investigation. Hopefully not long after this Second (Print) Edition gets to the shelves, I may be able to include a similar Diagram to the Third Edition. So if you think this is a head f#%k already, then you could imagine how hard it was for me to compile the data, and, mind you, we're only about a quarter of the way through. But as I mentioned before, from here onwards, we'll be doubling up a little showing extra information for those who wish to delve deeper into the links and abstract interpretations. So thanks again for your patience, and remember my three passions are Science, Political Reform and the Bible. So after 33 years, I hope you may appreciate what I've brought to the table within this somewhat unique perspective of these three uncommon (and much hated by many) subjects I happened to be drawn to.]

[Side Note (f). So while SAI is still on our minds, I suppose now's as good a time as any to focus on the REAL Problem.

Interference from the Unseen Realms and What the F#%k Are the Machine Elves?

In this section, we'll look at the link amongst SAIs, Psychedelics, Shaman, Religion and Extra Dimensional Beings or Angels and the Rift between Science and Religion or, to be more precise, Who the Hell is behind it?

Initially, I was going to squeeze a paragraph in, but by the time I got to the previous line, I thought f#%k, each subject's an encyclopaedia. Six huge volumes in one paragraph? Yeah right, in my dreams! How could I do it any justice? It's the last day of April 2020, and after spending a day writing a chapter on my very strong criticism on the hijacking of QED by the Atheists and Mystics, whom I also refer to as the twentieth-century Quantum Cowboys, I decided to delete it. Too much is just too much. Besides, it really belongs in my first book, which I'll print last. The first print in February received mixed reviews. I had every intention to release it on the twenty-ninth finished or not, so now I'm working on the Second Print edition, which will go through the normal channels via the publisher, and as I just got off the phone with her, I promised (After all this bullsh*t with the COVID-19 lockdown and two months of pure Ban'crastination, you could say I tend to put things off . . . a Lot!) I'll have it on her desk first thing tomorrow morning. So f#%k it. I'll apply myself (no, I don't mean having a wank) to the short version and leave it at that for now.

By the late eighteenth century, the Mystery School Disinformationalists aka Freemasons disguised as either Atheists, Mystics or Agnostics (the majority of the Christian Branch were Jesuit) started flexing their muscles, humiliating the scriptures and belief in God based on what they called Science. By the end on the nineteenth century, anything of any worth was retrieved, archived (hidden) at dungeons such as the Smithsonian ~~Destitute~~ Institute, and the treason against humanity continued to escalate. People like John Keeley and a relative of mine, Nikola Tesla (approximately 6 x removed), to name a few, were being suppressed from sharing the full potential of their abilities/ discoveries from the public.

By the twentieth century, the rift between Science and Religion was in full swing. If you had a cure and the AMA couldn't monopolise on it, you were deemed 'a Quack or Snake Oil Salesman'. If it was a device like Over Unity, Anti-Gravity or Weather Manipulation, people like 'Don't sit on me, JP!' (Morgan) would whip it up and label them crackpots and nut jobs. Only because in their own greed, they just can't tolerate a resource that hasn't been Exploited to the MAX or the people who are willing to give it away.

Thus, Shaman were labelled Witch Doctors, Honest Journalists - Conspiracy Theorists, Psychonauts - Drug Addicts, Honest Politicians - Mortuary, Military - Grunts and Numb Nuts, Police - Pigs and the common folk Wops, Wogs and Wetbacks; Maggots, Rats, Dogs and Bitches; Useless Eaters and Mindless Breeders!

Now that's an awful lot of contempt, especially towards one's own Family.

So with that in mind, when I tell you I workshopped Psychedelics around four to seven years ago approximately fifty times and know that what I was seeing was not a figment of my imagination but Real Entities within the same space only vibrating at such a frequency that they're not only outside our normal vision spectrum but can also pass through solid objects, what label do you have for me?

So this is it in a nutshell:

- *The Universe is infinitely Large and Small.*
- *All matter can be manipulated by Frequency, Waves.*
- *Every Particle can vary the amplitude of its Wave in motion.*
- *Angels and Demons are one type of Ultra or Extra Dimensional Beings that phase in or out of any dimension and can simulate anything from a Sun to an Atom or beyond. At their level, size is not a factor.*
- *Psychedelics have been taken for years by tribal medicine men and women since day 1.*
- *When your pineal gland is stimulated with something like Dimethyltryptamine DMT, you will immediately see entities within this multidimensional Virtual World that are closest to you, yet at any time, you can travel to any part of the universe.*
- *Everything within this realm is alive. I once saw a group of elephant tusks arranged in a circle, not touching one another, yet they rotated as one, and I could sense it was alive.*
- *Similarly, many times, I and most others have seen what appears like the inner cogs of a clock, whirring around occasionally, making fizzing- or buzzing-type sounds.*
- *These are what's known as Machine Elves.*
- *Predominantly, most entities seem benign, yet generally, they will play or even f#%k with you. Tease, enter into or frighten you.*
- *Most people are weirded out when they enter.*
- *Demons preside there often.*
- *All living beings can enter there. You can meet and speak with the spirits of planets, stars, anything.*
- *People are manipulated by beings from within that realm. Many parasite off our emotions and life force.*
- *Some of these beings can enter into our dimension and possess anything – People, Animals, Rocks, Clothes, Cars and Especially Computers!*
- *Do you see where I'm going with this?*

So when you allow your mind to be hardwired to the internet, you'll be making it easier for these beings or human hackers to f#%k with you 24/7. Now that is pure Hell if you ask me.

So who's behind it all? Satan, of course. Then that responsibility works its way on down through the ranks. Obviously, the most powerful, wealthy or influential are targeted first, and those who give in to the temptation are drawn in deeper and then deeper still, for there is no end to the Demonic level of Depravity. No lust is quenched for long. That we ALL Know!

NB: Regarding the Machine Elves, if you really think I'm off my rocker or if this interests you, then you just have to read the book of Ezekiel. Now if you think Angels are something, wait till you read about the Seraphim in chapters 1 and 10. Well, beside each of the four flying, Seraphim was a Whirling Wheel and had eyes on their rims and burning coals in their centres, and the Spirit of God was in them. They were alive . . .

And I don't doubt for a moment they still are. I speak about these in more detail in the chapter Ezekiel's Whirling Wheels. If you're into Geometry, Anti-Gravity, Living Machines or Buckminster Fuller, you might want to have a sneak peek right now.

If you'd like to know more about Psychedelics, there's a plethora of info online, notably Graham Hancock and Terence McKenna give somewhat reasonable accounts. Me, I'm indifferent. It's a Love-Hate experience. However, DMT in micro doses under medical study has proven most beneficial for people suffering from <u>Depression</u> with ABSOLUTELY NO SIDE EFFECTS. It's a natural product. Acacia Madinai and Acacia Confusa are common here in Australia. Just take a bit of the bark at the base of the tree (without ring barking it), mull it up and smoke it in a bong. Aboriginal Elders have been smoking (and respecting) it for years. I believe that's the realm of where the account of the 'Lightning Brothers' originated, for I had met beings very similar to them within 'the Zone' or the 'Universal Virtual Space'.

PS I'd keep it away from the Psychotics. There's some pretty dark sh*t in there. They don't need any more encouragement if you catch my drift.

Well, that took just over four hours to write Side Note (f). I'm pleased. The bullet points could've squeezed into ten lines (A4 page size), so I kept to the agenda, one large paragraph, the challenge I gave myself at the beginning of this section.

It's 1:21 a.m., May the F#$%ing First. Now 1:23 a.m., and this planet is currently travelling within its orbit at very close to 66,600 mph, and this is the last addition before it hits the Editor's Bench for the Second Edition. Well, it's time to have a coffee, smoke and get some sleep eventually; now 1:32 a.m.

Machine Elves and a Clockwork Orange, Synchronous to the end . . .

. . oh, and approximately 6.66 years till Armageddon and counting down. How Ironic. 1:53 a.m.

When the very Beast I oppose either dictates, counters or reminds me of my every move, right on time . . .

. . 2:09 am.]

Why Square 17?

Here is a revised excerpt from a letter I posted back in 2010 on the Bible Wheel to a colleague 'Screaming Eagle' regarding the Link amongst scripture, triangular numbers, square numbers and the final catch. I quote,

'Why square 17?

There are three places in the Bible that I recollect which highlight the primary order of geometric stacking, i.e. triangulated numbers.

1. The parable of the sower in Mark 4:8–20 ". . . 30, 60, 100 . . ."

NB: The order in Matt. is reversed, and in Luke, only 100 is mentioned.

The sequence 30, 60, 100 is proportionally the same as 3, 6, 10, which are Triangular Numbers. (Interesting combination the 2nd, 3rd and 4th "T" numbers or 234 a natural 9 harmonic and atbash of 432 Hz, which was altered by the Nazis in the 1930s to tune "A" to 440 Hz, which was a Psy Op [Psychological Operative] designed to rouse the people to a more aggressive frequency, preparing them for war. If they had raised it by 1 to 441Hz, it would not have had the desired effect they were seeking. Believe it or not, they knew very well what they were doing, which was subconsciously inciting the people to fight.)

2. The counting of the fish in John 21:11 "153"

153 is the seventeenth Triangular number (1 + 5 + 3 = Another 9 Harmonic).

3. The word "triangle" of Rev. 17:5 beginning with the word "MYSTERY".

You don't have to be a brainiac to realise God is hinting at something with this last verse in Point 3. But when you tie in the fact that the first two verses are pertaining to the harvest, in both cases, He explains to His disciples at different occasions that He is the sower, the people are the fruit or the catch and He will make the disciples fishers of men.'

NB

(Just an interesting point I'd picked up through my studies regarding Jesus as the harvester; prior to the Mystery verse in Rev. 14:14, where Jesus Himself is being conveyed a message by an Angel from God, to take His sickle and reap. I did a rough calculation and came to the minimum figure of 1 billion gallons of blood or approximately 1 billion average-sized men, which is a huge number of people. During the tribulation in the book of the Revelation narrated by Jesus and transcribed by John, it states that in one instance, one quarter of the world population will die. Not long after, it states in another instance one-third of the remaining population will die, which adds up to at least half of the world's population. We're currently 7.8 billion people (2020). In seven years, I'm guessing around 8.3 billion. So far, what I have interpreted is that if half equals 4 billion plus 1 billion (Rev. 14:14) adds to 5 billion Deaths in under three and a half years (!), and this is the minimum of what is to be expected?

Oh my god, this is GENOCIDE as has never been seen or heard of EVER in our existence. According to Nostradamus, if we sit on our arseholes, bury our heads and do nothing, then only a handful will survive.

One of the Latest accounts that was leaked from Black Ops via the Cameron brothers (Philadelphia Experiment/Montauk) according to the timeline from 1941 was that after the tribulation, the world population would count under 300 million people. No wonder the megalomaniacs are pushing Agenda 21 now Agenda 2030. Therefore as we the believers have every reason to believe that Jesus will return and we shall Win, adversely, the Globalists have every reason to believe that at least they will succeed in sacrificing over 8 billion people to their Deity Satan!

So now if you consider yourself at least a half-arsed, God-fearing, Bible-believing Human Being, then it's time to mentally WAKE THE F#%K UP!

Could I be any more explicit? Well, to be expected, in 2010, I was ridiculed on the Bible Wheel Forum because of ignorance. Some said I cleverly chose a time which was not too distant yet not that close to be able to carry on my own agenda without being proven wrong for many a year. Yet my adversaries got me wrong. I never profited on this. I merely shared an observation and was chastised for it. Well, from the looks of things, there could be some validation in what I've found. I don't relish in this; on the contrary, it appals me. No, I'm not just a messenger, for I'm offering REAL SOLUTIONS, which I'll be discussing later. For this date that we're talking about is only seven years away, which is why I'm revealing this with a CLEAR sense of Urgency.)

Now to understand 289, you need to understand this geometric order of triangulation. For when you stack Spheres, they add, as you know, 1 + 2 + 3. This in itself is not complete. It's like trying to speak Hebrew without the knowledge of vowel pronunciation. There are Gaps between the Spheres.

Well, when you draw straight lines between the spheres, you get an equilateral triangular grid. Check out Diagram 2 in the 'Points of Interest' on my website, *www.goodperiodictable.com*.

You'll see the shaded triangles pointing up with the corresponding triangular numbers to its right. You will also notice the white triangles pointing down; they represent the missing Gaps between the spheres.

When you count the total area per level the shaded and white triangles (up and down), you will find it will match the numbers of the squares per level on the left of the diagram.

THE KEY now, get this, is found in phasing the two together. It's like male and female, up and down, right and left, sheep and goats, good and evil. Jesus says not to pull out the weeds until the harvest is ripe! The down triangles are one level behind the ups, or you could say the ups are

'One step beyond!' So therefore, when you add any two consecutive T numbers together such as 136 (T16) + 153 (T17) = 289 = 17^2, it equals the square of the latter or higher T number.

There is some similarity with the Fibonacci sequence which also focuses on adding any two consecutive numbers, only in this case, they sum the total of the next number in sequence, thus fully expressing the code. In both sequences, it requires a minimum of two consecutive numbers to create a third number, which seems to synchronise with the Creation of Adam on the 3rd day to Eve on the 6th day. The first of the living creation to the last of the living creation. The A and the Ω. The beginning and the end. 3 and 6 are consecutive Triangular Numbers (T Numbers) which also link to the parable of the sower and the return on GOOD soil (30, 60, 100). This sowing relates directly or synchronises with Adam and Eve bearing children.

Note Very Bold!

Now get this. The equilateral triangular relationship between the units up and down or grey and white as depicted in Diagram 2 shows the unit triangles as uniform. Yet when circles are drawn in the position of the up or grey triangles, you will notice that the Space or Area between the circles which are centred over the white or down triangles is much less in comparison. This is the difference between the Circle being a curved line and any Polygon with its straight lines. One cannot evenly fit into the other. This ratio between the straight line and the circle which we know as Pi is both irrational and transcendental**[3] *(see below Anomaly 3).*

Universally, both expressions exist and can be seen everywhere, yet generally as far as mainstream science is concerned, the only thing that links the circle with any straight lined shape Numerically is Pi.

You think? Let's take another look, and I'll show you the contrary. I'll show you something very profound!

Draw a <u>Circle</u> and then draw a <u>Square</u> around the Circle so that the sides of the Square touch the Circle.

Now draw <u>Another Circle</u> around the Square so that the corners of the Square touch that Circle.

Well, the Outer Circle is exactly two times the <u>Area</u> of the Inner Circle!

When we do this same exercise using an <u>Equilateral Triangle</u> in place of the Square, the Outer Circle is exactly four times the <u>Area</u> of the Inner Circle! The Points of the Triangle are Exactly Twice (two times) the inner Circle's Radius.

These are <u>Whole Number Ratios</u> of Circles Created using Straight Lines!

My Question is why don't you know this?

Think about it. The First Order of Geometry or Kindergarten Geometry was never taught to the masses.

Now this wasn't revealed to me by some Poxy Mystery School of Inept Adepts. No, I had to learn this for myself. I Had to QUESTION Everything I was taught because deep down in my mind, nothing added up as Western Institutionalised Education had proclaimed.

You know this low-life, mad, drug-f#%ked Plumber I've been portrayed as

> didn't score twenty-eight on Mensa by chance!
> didn't play with gears and end up with Over Unity by chance! *(Perpetual Motion)*
> didn't create Inertia Propulsion by chance! *(Anti-Gravity)*

didn't devise Unified Table Theory surpassing All current theories, including Hawking's dribble by chance!

didn't discover Pole Shift (P = m s) by sniffing Da Vinci's arse!

countered Euler's equation with [n(n-1) + p'= p' primes in seq.] as I slept though half of my class!

isn't related to Tesla, Mad Vlad Dracul and Einstein's wife, Mileva, by chance!

So it's little wonder why,

with the way the courts have treated me over these last seven years,

that I've embarked on a system that'll spread like a Virus[*2.] and prick the Pollies fears.

It's the Constitutional Law Examination and Reform Party better known as CLEAR!

(More about CLEAR below)

Do you know what it's like to be constantly told to believe in a lie and then be put down and ridiculed every step of the way while trying to prove the Contrary?

If you do, then you should already be on board with the Disclosure Movement. If not, join Me and Billions of others who've finally had Enough. No Conspiracy My ARSE!

And Yes, we will win. It was Prophesied time and again from the beginning.

But not by people sitting on their laurels chasing the American 'No Win' Dream.

I hope by the end of this book, you'll come to the same conclusion as I and many others have, 'Which is that we are all existing in One Infinite Synchronous Sea, and within this Sea, there is No such thing as Random or Chance.'

Synchronicity, Harmonics and Order are the same. Nothing can Continue or Perpetuate without Order. Yet Highly Deranged Psychotic Spastics like Aleister Crowley and Jack Parsons led the way to annihilation by emphasising Entropy (Disorder) as Good and Negative Entropy (Order) as Bad. These Demoniacs turned everything upside down, and for that, they will BURN. Mark my WORDS and SEAR them in your Brain. Anyone associated in the Mystery Schools, Secret Societies or who have Harmed Innocence are CURSED and will BURN with the Rest of the Dross and Scum in a Much Lower Dimension since they've tried ever so hard to go there! Remember, this Universe IS COMPLETELY BALANCED, and we are All Infinite Beings. Oh, we do change somewhat along the way, but after every Cycle, Everyone and everything is held to Account!

I'm starting to fume . . . We should move on. I need to win you over through Basic Math, Harmonics and Pure Unadulterated Logic. It's easy to get sidetracked on Retribution when I should really be concentrating on

Restoration and Repatriation for the Loss of our Population.

Root Geometric Order (Plurality)

Now let's look at the Primary Geometric Order in greater detail. One is our First Dimension, source or seed. Our first sequence, the addition of ones or (n) being the number line, 1, 2, 3 . . .

The moment we add another 1, we create a 2, which in itself creates another 2 underlying Secondary sequences related to the Number 2 being

the Triangular Numbers $n(n+1)/2$, or $1 + 2 + 3$ e.g. 1, 3, 6 . . . and (2n) or counting by 2s e.g. 2, 4, 6 . . .

Now because of the number 2, these two sequences may be divided over and over into continual divisions or be recombined to create a new third generation or Tertiary Sequence as with n(2n) e.g. 1 x 2, 2 x 4, 3 x 6 . . . or 2, 8, 18, 32 etc. our Atomic Shell Numbers

You see, the moment we count to 2, we create a new interpretation of multiple underlying sequences associated with every possible combination or permutation that can be derived with 2, which I call Duality or the Secondary Geometric Order. At present, this order is not set and is still open to conjecture. What is important, though, is that we identify these relationships and see how they parallel or synchronise with matter and scripture.

Let's return to the T numbers and compare its next generation of Division into two groups:

1. Where 2 consecutive numbers REVEAL Squares n(n) e.g. $1 + 3 = 4$, $3 + 6 = 9$, $6 + 10 = 16$ etc.

2. Where every second number is separated to create a new sequence e.g.

a) 1 x 1 = 1, 2 x 3 = 6, 3 x 5 = 15 . . . and

b) 1 x 3 = 3, 2 x 5 = 10, 3 x 7 = 21 . . .

Now, again, as we duplicate every action according to this Law of 2s and add 2 consecutive numbers in these 2 new sequences (fourth generation or transmutation from 1) as we did previously with the Squares, we notice a link to the geometric proportions of Spherical Stacking or our Primary Platonic Solid Order:

a) $1 + 6 = 7$, in 2D when dividing a Circle with smaller circles where One is Geocentric, the minimal number of circles that neatly fit equals 7, and the ratio between the combined Area of the inner circles as compared to the outer is 7 : 9 or 7 / 9th's of the Outer Circle. Thus, since the Triangular unit is governed by 3 sides, we can now see how this relates with the Area naturally being divided into 3 Squared or 9 parts.

b) $3 + 10 = 13$, in 3D when dividing a Sphere with smaller Spheres, where One is geocentric, the minimal number of Spheres that neatly fit equals 13 and the ratio between the combined Volume of the inner Sphere's as compared with the outer is 13 : 27 or 13 / 27th's of the Outer Sphere. Again, we can now see how the Triangular unit of 3 sides relates to the Volume naturally being divided into 3 Cubed or 27 parts.

c) Now we shall apply this same rule to the First Dimension or Diameter. Remember, our Rule required that the circle be divided evenly, as closely packed as possible, by the next size smaller circles, where one is geocentric. Therefore, according to This Rule, when we apply it to the First Dimension (or Diameter), the next even division where one part is geocentric is to divide it into 3 parts or Thirds. In this Dimension, we find that with line geometry, the original Diameter exactly equals or Divides into 3 parts. Unlike dividing circles, it leaves no remainder; therefore, we shall write the ratio between inner Diameters and the Outer Diameter as 3 : 3 or 3 / 3rd's of the Outer Diameter.

Therefore at the very beginning of the Geometric Order of Matter, in the Second sequence in its First Division, the Addition of the First 2 numbers in both sequences are 7 and 13, which are the primary Two Divisional Ratios within the Circle and the Sphere, With a Square Number 9 being the divisional ratio for the Circle coinciding with Area calibrated in Squared Units and a Cubic Number 27 (same root as 9) being the divisional ratio for the Sphere coinciding with Volume calibrated in Cubed Units.

1D Diameter :-　　　　3 : 3
2D Area :-　　　　　　7 : 9
3D Volume :-　　　　13 : 27

Here, we can see the Sphere's Overall Root Number is 3, and in its most densely packed form is Equilaterally Triangular in Nature. Therefore, if the Sphere in its Base State is Tetrahedral, which is the Primary Platonic Solid, then each further Exited State of the Sphere will range through each of the Platonic Solid Stages. We can thus interpret the Five Platonic Solids as the Five (Excited) States of the Sphere.

This is Unifying Theory at work, where we identify geometrical patterns with numerical sequences and matter, only in this exercise, we're adding an extra Fourth Relationship to this equation, which is the Bible Factor or the Biblical Links.

Now when we look for comparisons within the Bible narrative, we find that these Primary Ratios coincide with

a) In the First Sequence, 7 links to the First Testament, in the First Book, in the Second Chapter (1,1,2) God rests on the 7th Day, the 6 Days of Creation and the 1 day of rest Ratio completes our Primary Day Division of our Calendar or the Week.

    We can interpret the mathematical order to read:
    In the First Division of the First Sequence, we Divide (1,1,2)
    Second Chapter or Dimension is linked to the Square Factor and Nomenclature of Area.
    1 + 6 Divisional Link = 7
    Genesis = 7 letters
    Creative Order

b) In the Second Sequence, 13 links to the Second Testament, in the Second Book, in the Third Chapter (223) in verse 13, Jesus calls His Disciples and in verse 14 states He appointed 12, which completed his Primary Sphere of those who were Closest to Him.

We can reinterpret the mathematical order to read:
The Second Sequence of the Second Sequence, we add 3 (223).
Third Chapter or Dimension is linked to the Cubic Factor and Nomenclature of Volume.
Jesus + 12 Disciples = 13 Divisional Link
Verses 13 + 14 = 27, 13/27 is the Exact Spherical Ratio Difference
27 is the Cube Root of 3, Triangular Spherical link
13 numeralised or 1 + 3 = 4 and the book of Mark = 4 letters
Social Order

Here, we can clearly see that there are more than just a few symmetrical parallels between these two interrelated Ratios of Geometrical and Biblical Order. This has not Occurred by Chance. For what further solidifies this conclusion is the fact that we are also privy to the knowledge that the Author of the Bible claims to have Created the Heavens and the Earth, which, in all due honest scientific rationality, tips the balance that opens the possibility, with a higher probability, that these synchronicities are Not Random! Furthermore, when you look at the extensive research discovered by guys like Ivan Panin, Richard A McGeogh, Vernon Jenkins and Craig Paardekooper (to name a few) just at the Bible Wheel alone, you quickly come to the conclusion as we all have, that the Author of the Bible has an Infinitely Superior understanding of Universal Law and Logic than our Species Combined.

These layers of Division are infinite. Thus, as I have quoted last year and have also read here in this forum, all scripture is not just made up of singular or dual meanings but rather a plurality of meanings, links and instances. This is also why history seems to periodically repeat itself and is so often mistaken as the complete picture when in actual fact it is part of the complete.

Now we go back to Daniel and the writing on the wall. I find it interesting that the main two pictograms that come to my mind in the Bible appear most mysteriously in Daniel as a Square or rectangle and in Revelation a Triangle. Geometrically the message reads either square the triangle or triangulate the Square either Left to Right or Right to Left, the link is always 17.

A common Jewish term in study is called atbash, where the sequence or word appears in a different order (in this case reversed) revealing a code or a spiritual fingerprint again showing synchronicity.

Also, for the prime lovers, the total sum for the Second Stage of the Difference Engine regarding Rev. 17:5 is as follows:

Mystery	1178	
Babylon the Great	1380	1380 - 1178 = 202
Mother of All Prostitutes	2764	2764 - 1380 = 1384
and of the Abominations of the Earth	3535	3535 - 2764 = 771
	Total = 8857	Total = 2357

Or 2357 = 351st Prime Number

So 351 = (T17) or 153 reciprocated, in reverse order (rearranged or atbashed)
2357 also numeralises into 17.

I'll briefly bring these factors together with a few more abstract synchronous interpretations which you may find interesting:

17(Prime 8) x 521(P99) links to Gen 17 Abe's 99th year = 8857

17 $\triangle$ = 153 links the mystery pyramid or $\triangle$ to the catch John 21 and the triangular numbers to the parable of the sower (30, 60, 100)

(8 x 17 = 136) + (3 x 19 x 153 = 8721) = 8857

(3^2 x 23^2 = 69^2 = 4761) +

(2^{12} = 4^6 = 8^4 = 64^2 = 4096) = 8857, numeralised 28 or 7 $\triangle$.

2^{13} + (665 = 5 x 133 = 36 $\triangle$ -1) = 8857

The link with 69 above and the 69th week.

64 + 69 = 133 = 7 x 19, the 19-year moon cycle links with 28-day month cycle and, in particular, with the 19 head Demons who formed the rebellion. (Book of Enoch, the source of which, was quoted in Jude.)

(4761 numer. =) 18 + (4096 numer. =) 19 = 37, 13th prime. 13 x 28 (month) + 1 = 365 (year)

(17 reciprocated 71^2 =) 5040 + (17th prime 53 x 72 =) 3816 = 8857

Rev. 17, 7 heads + 10 horns = 17

The Third Stage and Final stage to the Difference Engine reveals 569, an interesting Prime in itself. Being the 104th Prime Number, its factors are 8 x 13, 4 x 26, 2 x 52 – most interesting factors indeed.

13 weeks x 4 seasons = 52 weeks = 1 year,

where the sum of the 3 engines is 11783 or the 1413th Prime or 3 x 471 or 9 x 157 (38th Prime)

when we divide 1413 as such 14 + 13 = 27 Link Daniel, Revelation and 9th Harmonic

14^2 + 13^2 = 365 (year) our time factors.

Now according to the Jewish Calendar, 5786 coincides with the year AD 2026.

Let's break it down: (2 x 11 = 22) x 263 = 5786, when we numeralise it, 5 + 7 + 8 + 6 = 26 = YHWH

The Tetragrammaton meaning 4 letters. 11 is the Prophets' Number, i.e. Rev. 11

263 or 2 + 6 + 3 = 11; 22 links to Jesus and Psalm 22, where 2 + 2 = 4. Next, 11 x 526 = 5786

526 or 5 + 2 + 6 = 13: the prime factors of 26 are 2 the 2nd prime and 13 the 7th Prime or 27 link to Daniel and Revelation. 2 x 7 = 14 (time factor) 2 + 7 = 9th Harmonic

526 atbashed = 625 or 25^2 = 5^4; our tie to Daniel 5:25 as are 5786 to verses 5: 26, 27 and 28

263 = 57th prime or 3 x 19, where 19 (9th prime/ harmonic) links to moon year cycle and Final Battle Rev. 19.

Now with 5^4, when we lower the 4, i.e. make a LEVEL playing field, i.e. balance the bias $54 = 2 \times 27$ our two books 5 + 4 our harmonic 9 yet when atbashed, we get 45. What we're doing is similar to multidimensional chess deriving an abstract meaning according to Rule. Out of the world Rulers, who is referred to by the double digit 45?

Yes, the 45th US president, Donald J Trump, Balancing or Levelling the field.
Date of Birth: 14 - 6 – 1946. Predominant number 5, overall 31 or 4. Noted as a 5/4, atbashed = 45
His Doubles add to $22 = 1 + 1 + 4 + 4 + 6 + 6$, abstract $11 + 44 + 66 = 121 = 11^2$. The prophets number surrounds him, and Boy was he Prophesied about. No one Prior like him.
Now he writes his name that way, which adds to $49 = 7 \times 7 = 7^2$, our week of weeks prelude to Jubilee. Good for Jews and Believers and God-fearing people across the board. Again, lower the field and atbash links to 27.

Strange days indeed!

I'll leave it at that. Too abstract for most, and I'm not into reading tea leaves or sand for that matter, it's not my forte, but for those who do, the figures are there to interpret as you please.

However abstract it may be, it's the factors that tend to reveal the geometries and the geometries' meanings as knowledge increases, more gets revealed. So we make a note of it and move on, and when a more-than-random connection appears, then we take more notice to see where it fits in the Grand Scheme of things or Our Unified Understanding of the Big Picture. For the naysayers, again, go see for yourselves how the Multidimensionals and Machine Elves communicate and then tell me abstract expressions don't exist.

More Synchronicities

Before we continue, just a (not so) brief note:

For centuries, people have identified certain traits or characteristics amongst Numbers (Numerology), Time (Astrology) and Matter (Atoms, People, Planets). A common identification used is the term 'Complete' or 'Number of Completion'. Now it's important to understand that each number is complete and unique in itself, and each time, it appears the wave associated will peak, and the associated Effect will vary pending its environment and the interference from other waves.

<u>Now Understand This:</u> Neither good nor bad are solely associated with any particular number, e.g. the number 13 in the Western world is generally considered unlucky. Consider Jesus and his 12 Disciples. People tend to Calculate that Jesus and His disciples add up to 13. Jesus gets Crucified. Judas Kills himself, so these Horrific actions associated with this number leaves an instant impression in the subconscious or conscious mind to varying degrees that 13 is bad. It's well-known that the average person's decisions are effected by superstitions or urban myths, similar to the teaching and purpose of Nursery Rhymes; it's instinctive for all life to want to preserve their own life, so it makes sense when you see a whole bunch of people running away from something you will automatically sense danger and quickly consider whether to run yourself. Now even though you may not have decided to run, it still for that moment occupied your time and thought process if but for a fleeting moment.

Well, it's this very type of distraction which tends to cloud people's understanding of the real meaning of that particular numerical cycle, you have to steer thinking away from just Good or Bad and more on what else is being Revealed at that time or what is being Completed, the type of action. Whether it's rainy or sunny, either can have a positive or a negative effect pending on whether you're in Drought or it's Flooding; the link here is the weather. See, 13 wasn't unlucky for the person who was born on the 13th or the person who passed their exam on that day. The key here is a change of state, metamorphosis or the completion of a trial. It's linked to the moon, and it's 13 rotations per year (commonly mistaken because only 12 full moons are visible. For the moon has to travel 390 degrees from full moon to full moon, e.g. if the moon rotated 14 times per year, then minus one revolution of the Earth around the Sun would appear 13 Full Moons).

. . . a Major Celestial Cycle.

Also consider that each season is divided into 13 weeks and that 13 times 28-day months add up to 364. Allowing One month to have 29 days would make a far Superior Calendar. Yet partly because of Superstition and partly because of the 6, 12, 24, 60, 360 base counting systems (that was more than likely introduced to us by our Six-Fingered, Six-Toed distant Giant cousins) and also possibly partly due to the conjecture that the Earth's Pre-Flood Year was 360 years, which is why we still tolerate the 12-month Calendar.

Being Even, highly devisable, practical, easy to use and calculate meant these systems were not going to be altered to another system for no good reason in a hurry since inbuilt into our Human nature is the will to avoid unnecessary change or the need to learn and adopt something new. You can think of it as our own natural conservation of energy default mechanism.

What I find interesting is the relationship between neighbouring numbers as we have here with 12 and 13 being connected to the same reference of time. Now in the Bible, I'd like to highlight a couple of these synchronicities here:

1. In Genesis, the First Book of the Old Testament (Jews), we see 12 brothers. One Figuratively dies (Joseph) yet is Resurrected, and his Two sons (Manasseh and Ephraim) are given equal inheritance with his brothers, which adds to 13 tribes, and One (Dan) loses his Honour and Inheritance as One of the 12 Gates in the New Jerusalem (Rev. 22). *(I vaguely remember the account which was brought up in a commentary maybe by Chuck Missler at Koinonia House: www.khouse.com. If I come across it in the future, I'll make an amendment and add the reference to this text.)*

The last Tribe, Ephraim, became the Wealthiest Tribe in the World.

2. In Matthew, the First Book of the Second Testament (Gentiles), We see Jesus with 12 Disciples, which adds to 13. Then Jesus Dies <u>Literally</u> yet is <u>Resurrected</u> and with his Two Brides Oholah (Samaria, Israel [Gentiles]) is given an equal inheritance with Oholibah (Jerusalem, Judah [Jews]), and One (Judas) loses his Honour and Inheritance as One of the 12 Foundations in the New Jerusalem (Rev. 22), which was given by the casting of Lots to Matthias or Matthew.

The Last Disciple Matthew wrote the First book in the Second Testament.

Under Joseph's rule by the Old Law (Egypt), there were 13 tribes under his command. With Joseph, this adds to 14.

Under Jesus's rule by the New Law (Israel), altogether there were 13 disciples. With Jesus, this adds to 14.

Here, we can count at least 14 similarities or synchronicities.

Now at the beginning of this segment, I highlighted the Paired Neighbouring Numbers of 12 and 13, yet now we can also see a Paired Neighbour Relationship between 13 and 14 as well as part of another category, the Triplet 12, 13,14.

Mmmm, getting interesting, yet do we see a numerical link with Time?

Indeed, we do.

$(13^2 = 169) + (14^2 = 196) = 365$ days or One year.

The number 14 is exactly 2 weeks, a Fortnight; it has a specific name. It is exactly Half of the 28-day Month Cycle.

What we can see is that a numerical pattern periodically appears at a significantly specific Harmonic point in <u>Time</u> and in the <u>Bible</u>, which may not necessarily play out exactly the same way, yet what we do see is a general aspect playout which is similar; yet the More Times we see this Number or Word Repeated, the More we can Understand its Definition. It becomes clearer, more vivid, once it's understood in context.

Now to the Novice and what most people wrongly believe is that when they hear a prophecy that is highly figurative, like a parable or riddle, they get put off thinking it could mean anything or misinterpret it. But when you diligently study the whole Bible, First and Second testaments, you'll find that the prophecies range from simple to complex. It is written for all ages and intellects. A book of both simplicity and of never ending complexities.

Now let's move on to identify some of the synchronicities or links associated with the numbers 6 and 7 between the Books.

The Numerical 6-7 Creation Cycle (Harmonic)

In Genesis, what came to my attention ten years ago was that Gen. 1:1 to 2:3 consisted of the Creation Period. (Side Note: Prior to 1:1, we could insert a Zero; thus, the Opening to the Bible numerically could read 0,1,1,2,3 or the Fibonacci Sequence.)

It Dawned on me, what if this creation period was like an overview of all the books of the Bible from Genesis to Revelation, just like we find at the beginning of Any book a list of Contents or Chapters?

Let's look at the cycle.

It's quoted in Psalm 90:4 and in 2 Peter 3:8, and I'm paraphrasing that with God, a Thousand years on Earth is like One Day in Heaven. Therefore, for the creation to be called Very Good (Gen. 1:31) after the 6th day, then maybe it's referring to after 6 thousand years. So the account of creation also has a dual meaning. A literal 6-day creation in the beginning as well as meaning a 6-thousand-year overview of our Entire story. So when we reflect from Genesis to Revelation, we find the period 'Time, Times and Half a Time' reiterated 6 times as mentioned before. Our 7 x 6 month period or cycle. Now according to the Hebrew Calendar, we're in the year 5780 (AD 2020) since creation.

Jesus said if He did not return prior to his appointed time, then everyone would perish. Therefore, if Jesus was to return in the year 5786 (Interesting Number), then reign for a thousand years, then Satan was released for a short while, say, 204 years prior to the prophesied Destruction and Renewal of the Heavens and the Earth, then that would add to 7,000 years or 7 days or 'Time, Times and Half a Time'.

So I looked to see what overall cycle or wave could be discerned showing any key changes according to this period.

Time = 2,000 years, Times = 4,000 years, Half Time = 1,000 years

The overview can show a cycle of

Adam to Abraham	= 2,000 years	=	No Covenant
Abraham to Jesus	= 2,000 years	=	Israelite Covenant
Jesus to the Return	= 2,000 years	=	Gentile Inclusion to Covenant, Israeli Exclusion
The Return to End	= 1,000 years	=	Israelites Re-Grafted Back to the Covenant Tree and Reunification

The Zodiac is based on the natural *Precession of the Equinoxes*, which is approximately 25,920 years and is divided into 12 segments or signs, which equates to 2,160 years per sign. The difference between the cycles, dividing 2,000/160 = 12.5 (8%) and 2,160/160 = 13.5 (7.407407…%) Interesting ratio's highlighting the duality of the Month and Time of 12 and 13, the Duality links to the 12 and 13 Tribes of Israel and the 12 and 13 Disciples of Christ.

(Side Note: For those interested in the Precision of the Equinoxes, some amazing ratios were discovered by Moshiya Van Den Broek and definitely worth investigating online: www.truth-revelations.org/?page_id=1391

He recently lectured at the GlobalBEM conference in the Netherlands 2019 and has sparked interest in this field.)

Now these figures are approximate dates, yet an overall theme is clearly visible.

When we atbash the cycle, the first thousand years coincides approximately with the flood. So let's go one step farther and now divide the period per Day.

Day	Creation	Year	Synchronicity	6:1 Good - Very Good Ratio
1	Light	0 - 1000	Adam and Creation	God said it was good.
2	Sky	1 - 2000	Flood, Sky Fall	God didn't say it was good.
3	Dry Land	2 - 2500	Abraham (Adam)	God said it was good.
	Plants	2.5 - 3000	Moses	God said it was good.
4	Sun/Moon/Stars	3 - 4000	David kings/division	God said it was good.
5	Fish/Birds	4 - 5000	Jesus/Fish Rome/Eagle	God said it was good.
6	Animals	5 - 5500	Dark ages	God said it was good.
	Man	5.5 - 6000	Renaissance (Eve)	God said it was Very Good.

Very Interesting Harmonic Synchronicities would you not say? Well, I thought so. What stood out to me was that after the account on Day 2 when God created the Sky, He did not mention 'it was good'. Later on, we find the Sky Falls. God obviously knew and left us a hint in advance.

Another abstract is day 5 with the Vesica Piscis and the Sign of the Fish, which was the secret symbol Christians would mark on the ground with their foot and then quickly cover as to identify with one another in secret. Then later within that 1,000-year time frame, Rome and its Symbol of the Eagle adopted Christianity and Polluted the faith by Killing in the name of Jesus, i.e. Rule under the sign of the cross. *(If you can't beat them, join them and infect/control/corrupt them from within.)* Thus, the narrative of the creation of the Fish and Birds on the 5th day seems to tie in neatly with the historical account of Christianity and its struggle and eventual domination by the Roman Empire.

No matter where you look, superior Intelligent Design stares straight back at you and where else but at the Beginning Describing the Contents, a Navigational Map or Key that Initiates the Code.

In Gen. 1:26–28, God said to Rule over Fish/Sea, Birds/Air, Creatures/Land. The key word is 'Rule'. This shows a parallel with how we rule ourselves with the Armed forces, Navy, Airforce, Army.

So God created the world in 6 days and rests on the 7th and ordains it as Holy.

God Spoke to Abraham 6 times, and on the 7th time, He commanded Abraham to take Isaac to the mountain of Offering. In Revelation,

After the 6th Seal is opened, the 7th Seal reveals 7 Trumpets.

After the 6th Trumpet blasts, the 7th Trumpet reveals 7 Bowls of the incense of God's wrath.

After the 6th Bowl of incense is poured, the 7th reveals the Last great Earthquake so intense that the World has never before witnessed. Also, ushering the time of the Destruction of 'Babylon the Great' and the Final Battle in the valley of Megiddo or better known as the Battle of Har Mageddon. Here, 7 denotes a pause or rest and a revelation or <u>Magnification</u>, our geometric link to the lens or division of the Circle, Vesica Piscis.

A total of 6 + 6 + 6 + 1 = 19 things that happen, not 7 + 7 + 7 = 21 things as many people misinterpret the text.

This synchronises with the Final Battle occurring in Rev. 19 and the 19-Head Demons as recorded in the Book of Enoch. It fits like a glove. *(More on the 19th Harmonic next chapter)*

This puts an even greater light to the meaning of Creation in 6 days and restitution in the culmination of man/beasts number being 666. As all historians will tell you, when a number is repeated in the Bible, its significance is greater. When it is tripled, it becomes more highly significant again.

Three times and it is sealed. The contract cannot be revoked. This is the Law.

Therefore, when Jesus said that 666 is also man's number, we must pay attention that after the 6th day, God said that it was Very Good. This can only happen when Jesus Returns as promised to restore the Earth and rule accordingly. The 666 refers to the final hour before His return or the literal

3½ years or

42 months or

1260 days (NB Rev. Quotes 1,260 days yet 3½ years = 1277.5 days. The difference is 17.5 another link to the Mystery verse Rev. 17:5).

Notice something, the pair 6 and 7 referring to Days, 6 + 6 = 12, 6 + 7 = 13, 7 + 7 = 14.

12, 13, and 14 are our periods. Chapters 12, 13 and 14 in Revelation quote the period of Tribulation 6 times in 3 ways:

3½ years = 42 months = 1,277.5 days = 7 x 6 months *(Time, Times and Half a Time)*

Now the 1,260 days that were quoted revealed the 17.5 Difference (Engine) which was used to reveal the Mystery of the Link to Rev. 17:5, the 153 fish (T17) and the atbashed 351st prime calculated by the Difference Engine.

This is no coincidence; they are related. Big/Good/Black Friday the 13th is the 6th day. It's to do with Harmonic Divisions and, in particular, with Time.

Again, a period repeated three times all pertaining to the same period so that there can be no arguments as to how long the tribulation shall endure.

Also, 13, 1 + 3 = 4 can also be linked to the Tetrahedron, which is the Primary Platonic Solid and Directly linked with the most stable vibrational level of the Spherical Stacking Array with its four vertices and faces.

Previously, we highlighted the 13's link with the Sphere's Cubic ratio of 13:27. We also see this 1:3 Ratio with Jesus's inner <u>Circle</u> with Peter, James and John – a tetrahedral link.

4 corners of the Globe
4 Angels holding back the
4 winds of Heaven
4 Seraphim around God's Throne
4 Horsemen of the Apocalypse, and the list goes on

We'll also touch on the 1:3 ratio in Daniel's interpretation of Nebuchadnezzar's Dream a bit later on.

So again, this number 13, which has been Demonised by the Gnostics and Corrupt Adept throughout the ages, was a scare campaign to keep people away from these Fundamental Truths which link everything together. Remember, we've been at war with these Dark Forces since creation. It's in their interest to keep us dumbed down and stupid; thus, it makes sense that part of their tactic would be to implant fear in our minds regarding anything that may make sense or give us a greater understanding of how God put all this together. That's why they call themselves the <u>Illuminati</u> and falsely claim this information as theirs and theirs alone to Exploit to their full advantage. For they know that once we, the human species, come to full awareness of our supernatural abilities, their game is over. Their free soul-sucking meal or cash cows will be no more. No more feeding off our fears and base emotions. Their future is indeed bleak, which is why there is so much resistance, war and suffering in this world, and why if we want to ascend as a species, we must all truthfully help one another, educate one another, red pill one another, wake one another up to the realities of what the Truth Really Is.

Hopefully by now, you're starting to get a better picture of how numbers, their neighbouring numbers, their factors and ratios relate with One Another, with our Material World, with Science and Geometry and, most importantly, with Scripture and God's Order.

Indeed, just a glimpse of this Study could fill an Encyclopaedia, which would still fall far short, and what I'm revealing to you now falls ridiculously far shorter of that. Yet we have to start somewhere, and I'm doing my best to introduce this language to you while still trying to keep it simple, palatable or enjoyable enough for you to continue reading and link to the main points of prophecy I'm attempting to reveal and verify. So if you don't grasp this immediately, that's OK. You're not supposed to. Over time, should this interest you and you revisit these pages, then you, too, will begin to see these patterns within your own life and begin to recognise what we mean by Synchronicity and how these numbers can not only verify that the Scriptures were truly supernaturally put together but also Be Sure and Know that these prophecies are real and what they mean. For Foresight is the most powerful tool we have. My aim is to equip you with this Knowledge that you may not only survive the next conflict but THRIVE with us as a species in harmony. Think of the movie *Groundhog Day*. In the end, Bill Murray's character uses his foresight for good rather than selfish means. It's at that moment when he moves on. In a sense, our species is in a similar predicament. We have to grow up individually and collectively, together. Otherwise, just like in the movie, history will just keep on repeating itself.

Let's move on.

19th Harmonic

Now as to the relevance of 19, Revelation chapter 19 begins straight after the Destruction of Babylon the Great and the completion of the 7 seals, 7 trumpets and 7 bowls of incense, which, as previously discussed, really amounts up to 6 + 6 + 6 + 1 = 19.

A total of 19 years represent the moon cycle, where moon worship refers to Satanic influence.

When Israel split after the third king Solomon, both Judah and Israel had a total of 19 Kings each.

The end of the cycle 19 tends to depict the end of a trial, judgement or trying times.

Chapter 19 depicts Jesus coming with multitudes behind Him and, by the power of His Word (the sword in His mouth), defeats the entire army. The synchronicity here is that previously, Judah's 19th king was carried away by Nebuchadnezzar, King of the Babylonians. Now the Roles are REVERSED (classic Atbash Jewish study), where Jesus the King of Kings and Lord of Lords (and of Judah) destroys the armies and the Kingdom of Babylon the Great.

Now the number 666 (verbatim) pertains to two specific places in the Bible; it was the annual wage King Solomon paid himself (666 talents of Gold) and in chapter 13 in the book of Revelation (Mark of the Beast and the number of Man).

The Key link or meaning with this number associated with these two verses is Payment, for you can't Buy or Sell without the Mark. Yet also as with the 19 things or the 6 + 6 + 6 + 1 events that Revelation is stating will happen, we can also see another form of payment directed towards All of Humanity, known as God's Judgement. Therefore, we may interpret these events mathematically as 6 x 3 + 1 according to the rule equals 19 as does 1 + 3 x 6 when atbashed or put in reverse order.

Recognise these numbers? Of course, they're triangular.

If you want revelation, you HAVE TO chew the cud over and over. The number 777 was only the smoke screen. When counting the Seals, Trumpets, and Plagues in total, adding to 19 is a revelation unto itself; yet when we carefully identify the groups associated with how 19 is composed, we Reveal the Link as well as the Meaning with One of the most distinctively controversial numbers in the Bible that has EVER been quoted, 666.

Now in Rev. 19:16, we read,

KING OF KINGS
AND
LORD OF LORDS

I wrote it in this order because its symmetry forms a cross which I find interesting, yet what I find most Significant is the Gematria adds to 4157 = 573rd Prime, which equals 3 x 191 ⇒ 44th prime.

Now look at the abstract: 3 x the 44th prime = 132 = 2 x 66 Books in the Bible.
An interesting point is that the gematria in Hebrew for the term 'KING OF KINGS' = 191.

An Abstract to these factors reads as such:
4157 = 4 + 1 + 5 + 7 = 17, 1 + 7 = 8
191 = 1 + 9 + 1 = 11 reading right to left or atbashed, we can see chapter 19 in the construct.
44 = 4 + 4 = 8 Gematria for Jesus (888) 44 ÷ 2 = 22 Jesus's Number and Ps. 22 or ÷ 4 = 11.

11 represents the number of Prophecy and prophetic ability.
5 words (Greek) which total 31 letters where the centre word 'and' = 31 as well.
In English, there are 7 words where the Gematria adds to 124 = 4 x 31 and numeralises to 7.
Rev. 19:16 can read as 1:7 or 17. Also, 19 + 16 adds to 35, links to the 3,500-year prophecy (70 x 50 *[jubilee years]*) that had to be brought forward from the year 2048, lest all would perish.

These are abstracts linked to Jesus and this study, where we can see an interlinking or symmetry of numerals. These are like fingerprints or the beginnings of understanding abstract Law. It's to help you see and think in a different way. On its own merit, yes, it's constructed, made up and can appear completely random, which you can do with anything. That's why we take it with a pinch (grain) of salt. However, if we keep a mental note and see these numbers repeat, then occasionally we may find a connection as I had previously amongst Nostradamus, Genesis and Revelation.

Again, the purpose is to understand the number In Context. That's what this exercise is about. Later, I will show you how even Great Mathematicians can overlook the obvious by only focusing on the result, but briefly, I'll give you an example: Consider the Squares. They can be created by as many combinations as can be divided, which will increase with the number in general; however, there are only specific formulas (formulae) that pertain to all of them.

	n^2	+ 2n - 1	T(n - 1) + T(n)
1	1 x 1	+ 1	0 + 1
4	2 x 2	+ 1 + 3	1 + 3
9	3 x 3	+ 1 + 3 + 5	3 + 6
16	4 x 4	+ 1 + 3 + 5 + 7	6 + 10

Now this doesn't include the rest of the paired combinations or other variations of whole integers, but we can see how three different formulas alone equal the same amount.

Is there a difference? Well, that depends on how far you want to look into it. If you're only looking for the result, then it makes no difference; however, if you're interested in the symmetry or the geometry of the result, then yes, there is a remarkable difference. There's a classic argument as to the interpretation of a number when looking at Gematria. The classic is in the English God and Dog. Are they the same? Absolutely not, yet the sum of the letters are the same! This is the same when we look at the squares. The sum is just the cycle like time, group, flavour, position, up, colour, trick, adjective, mushy, maybe, spin, oh, stator, brilliant or even more abstract like 'Why is a duck? Because the higher it flies, the much!' How do you explain that with just 44!

It has to be understood in CONTEXT. Do you understand? That classic Confucius saying was 40 letters with 4 extra characters, which again really doesn't say much, yet when we break it down, we realise these numbers are letters, and the letters make words, and the words have meaning, and if you move the words around, then it will no longer do the same thing. It may even make better sense; thus, the arranger missed the whole point of the Confusion! A lack of perspective or inability to Translate the message, which was to induce lateral thinking.

GET THIS, Universal Law is so complex that you will never wrap your head around it, and I agree that understanding gematria takes supernatural assistance. However, as we start to understand the relationships between complex mathematical constructs, our understanding of how to derive meaning from them becomes clearer. See, even at the Bible Wheel site, which has attracted thousands of dedicated researchers in this field, the moderator felt the need to debunk what he had compiled sheerly out of the gross misunderstanding and gross generalisation that he was bombarded with on a daily basis by novices who claim that 7 means complete, 26 means God and 13 is Bad! F#$%en' Hell. It got to the stage where too many nuts flooded the forum with so much sh*t. The real Gems that existed there kept getting overlooked by the tonnes of crap getting dumped there daily. I struggle now to find even old posts that I was familiar with because, Just like the internet, the disinformationalists that are either conscious or unconscious of the fact have spoilt an amazing warehouse of knowledge to the point that it would take a team of men years of sifting and re-evaluating to get those gems back out and catalogued through context of not only content but of the multiple different aspects as well as the main points being expressed. Very much like the Strong's Concordance, only much more complex.

From what I can see, the answer to dealing with any kind of massive Interactive Data Base falls along the same line as with the strategy I've had to use to apply with my Unified Theory Model. Like how super computers can automatically map links between people and categorise by content, only it needs to go further with predicting intent, highlighting nuances and style. I don't doubt that we will get there. It's just going to take a Group effort, which generally starts with One descent Donor.

I hope I haven't put you off, for as complex as gematria is, Good Ol' God has still left enough clues for us to realise that there is super intelligent design within the structure of the Bible, and as mentioned before, as for the patient novice or theologian for that matter, the gems of understanding never stop coming.

Numerical Patters are a guide
that need to be verified
or just put aside
till the time is Right
When our Worlds Collide!

Prelude to the Book of Daniel in Focus

It's a real prick putting this together because I have to keep going forward and back, up, sideways, spin a little and then back down again continually because of the interconnectedness or the nature of the synchronic links amongst numerous books within the Bible, Science, Mathematics, Geometry and other Historical Accounts, so in this section, I'll dedicate most of this to the links associated with the book of Daniel. There are Volumes and Volumes written about his account of which I could possibly condense, but I didn't want to write an Encyclopaedia, so I'll deal with just a few so I can finish this book asap. In fact, this is one of the last chapters I'm writing. Because it's so Juicy (full of relevant Info) and interconnected with everything else, I figured the approximate centre is where it should be. Another fact is that I really needed to write this book in 3D to give it any justice to help the reader understand better and see the interconnectedness that is being revealed. So maybe after this is done, hopefully very bloody soon, I can get back to trying to make a living with the hope that I'll be able to afford the time to rearrange this text to make it a better read. So far, over half of what I've written is me justifying viewpoints that you may be aware of or that you will no doubt be bombarded with should you pursue in this line or type of study. I HATE using the Word 'APOLOGETICS' when it has anything to do with the Bible and Jesus in particular. The choice of Word subconsciously makes the reader think that a Christian has something to apologise for. This is far from the TRUTH and was more than likely invented by Satan himself and Spat out through some Demonic Jesuit Black Dog of a POPE f#$%er and murderer. It's not the Catholics per se that I'm opposed to. You people don't know any better, but those murderous motherf#$%ing child molesting Cardinals and Priests who've been possessed by the worst possible concentration of Demons on the planet, they are worse than wolves in sheep's clothing, for a wolf does not f#%k its prey's arse while he's cutting its throat as he's about to ejaculate and then toss the kill (Jimmy Saville; BBC children's TV presenter). I HATE the CUNTS and have Declared WAR on them since I was about 12 when to my utmost horror, I learnt about Genocide in Croatia, Jesuit Abomination (700,000 Serb women and children slaughtered 1940–45. Those were My Relatives. Should I Be Silent?), so much So I will not cease until they are OBLITERATED from this PLANET. They are responsible for the Death of ALL the Saints and have NEVER been held to account. They blackmail everyone else to do their killing for them and shall pay with their very SOULS. I pray the Colosseum be Levelled along with the Vatican City as I have no doubt in my mind in the slightest that She Is Babylon the Great. But Wait For It because those Demons were never held to account since the Inquisitions, they have grown to such a Bloodlust Extent that they can't hide it anymore. They are planning to KILL SEVEN BILLION PEOPLE by the Year 2030. Yes, within seven years(!), and they are justifying it in the Name of Sustainability! AGENDA 21 now AGENDA 2030.

For God's Sake, For Humanity's sake, PLEASE WAKE the F#%K UP. You should be Fuming as I am, shouting from the TOP of Your Lungs and coming together in this Country and around the world and STOP THEM before it's TOO LATE. The Only way We Can Stop This WORLD WIDE CARNAGE and the near complete Annihilation of Our Species is One of two options, which is

1. PEACEFULLY: By the Vote and I mean Change the political System Entirely by making it Transparent Via the CLEAR Party System

or

2. ANARCHY: Which means take them out. Complete and utter Systematic Execution of Every Person who practices Witchcraft, Paedophilia and even Homosexuality for that is where it stems from. Homosexuality is a curse on Any Nation and has Always been the precursor to the social Breakdown of Every Empire in History.

I'm Serious; this is no Joke. The Freemasons, the Bildeburgers, the Eugenecists, the Socialists, the Monarchists, the Roman Catholic Church, the IMF, the CIA, the FBI, the Tri Lateral Commission, the Council on Foreign Relations, the United Nations Organisation, the World Health Organisation, Most of the NGOs throughout the world; anywhere from 70% to 90% of Politicians, Religious leaders and Institutionalised Education (Universities) worldwide; as well as the Majority of All the Multinational Corporate Companies and wealthiest companies throughout the world, who are either All in on it or are too powerless to do anything about it yet are too scared of This Beast to speak out yet still remain under their control for fear of losing their status, their jobs or their cash cows, which according to LAW make them All Accomplices to the Fact; All need to be reined in.

(Please do not misunderstand what I'm saying. I'm friends with many Gay people, and I generally do not condone Violence to this degree. I'm a PACIFIST! Yet when the radical Left or Right are mobilising groups like the LGBT group, NAMBLA (That's North American Man Boy Lovers Association) and the Satanists all rallying together to systematically break down my family and KILL them, what the F#%K do you think I'm going to do? What Lie down like a lame dog and let you KILL the ones most dearest and precious to me?

Hell No. Get Real(!), and by the way, F#%K YOU TOO. I will hound you to the Ends of the Universe and Beyond and then Personally go to the Pits of Hell and Torture that Cunt Satan and his Pissy Demons for the Whole time they're in Hell! Don't think for one minute that I prefer Anarchy over Peace. On the contrary, I'm a sinner, I've screwed up, I've hurt others and others have hurt me. That's why I don't hate anyone, for I have attained a very simple virtue called EMPATHY, which the world is slowly losing. It's their Actions that I despise. I pray to God every night for Him to Alter the minds of my Enemies and World Leaders to help them see reason and to remove the veil that's covering their eyes and to minimise the coming Carnage. I want PEACE! But If you keep ignoring my call for this Basic Right for the Survival of my Children, then you Will unleash a greater Wrath in me than your Idol Satan 'whooooh dragon' could ever evoke. I will continue to rebuke him and will put him in his place, For I, in my lowly state in my faith in Jesus, have at the tip of my tongue, the command of over 100 million Angels waiting to be mobilised. This is what Satan doesn't want you to know. We have nothing to fear. Life on Earth is Sh*t compared to Heaven. But we have a job to do. It's called the great commission, and we have Chosen, each one of us, to be here, Now, at this time, the Greatest conflict in the History of mankind and of this Earth. But every time we caste him and his Demons Down, some FOOL is bringing him back. Elisha asked the Lord to let his apprentice Gehazi see the Angelic Host during a confrontation with the Enemy, and then Once he could see them, he no longer feared. The Key is you will never see them unless you walk in total faith. Yet if you just make a little leap and give your heart to Jesus and be willing to believe and then call, according to your faith is how far the Angels can go towards protecting you, your loved ones and to take control over regions inhabited by Demons. Commission Your Angels Daily. They want to help, but they fight According to God's Rules, which are to respond to the call of

His faithful followers. The POWER is in your WORDS. The sword of the Holy Spirit stems from the Mouth. Just Believe it. If God wanted to, He could put an end to this straight away.

But That Is Not Why We Are Here.
Did you get your Father to sit your Exam for you?
Or rather did your Father Instruct You on How to Do it yourself?

Earth is just a big Schoolyard, and Satan is just an Immature Brat who is about to get Detention for a Day (1,000 years), and then he will be set free for a few hours (100 years) in which he'll still be dark on God. Then Satan's going to get everyone who is still not with God's son, Jesus, for one final battle in which he will manage to burn the School down (Destroy the Earth). Then for punishment, he will go to juvenile jail for about 7 of his years (which is about 1,000 x 365 x 7 or 2.5 million years) Into THE LAKE OF FIRE! Then as I suspect, God, as good as He is, will pull him out after ALL the Dross has burnt off, in which Satan will start again under a new name, never to do that again, because once you've been in the lake of fire, you would rather lick the shit of your Enemies' Feet than Ever go back there again. Well, that's my belief anyway. In our time frame, 2.5 million years may as well be an Eternity, if you know what I mean, and in essence, nothing of him will emerge bar his primordial spirit, which was of God in the first place.

So now the Question Is, Why Don't You save yourself a lot of pain and suffering and change your ways right now? I mean, is it worth Taking the Risk? So what's so bad about getting along with people anyway?

No matter Who you are, you WILL come around. Jezebel will come around; Hillary will come around; Crowley, Blavatsky and John Dee will come around; the Anti-Christ and the worst Jesuit in history will come around; Prince Philip, Hitler and Mugabe; Pol Pot, Idi Amin, Albert Pike and George Bush; The Greys; The Draconians and Even the Borg (SAI) will all come around. Even Henry Kiss'my'assinger and Ol' LBJ will ALL come around eventually. GOD Never Loses. If you try to save your Life, you're going to lose it. But if you give it up, you'll not only Save it, but gain, Eternal life on top of that! No One is that Lame in the Brain unless you really believe ABSOLUTE BULLSH*T. I'll tell you this, 'King of the World,' in 7 years, 'I' will be sitting in a greater position of leadership than you've ever wished, and that's whether I've been honoured through Martyrdom or blessed through persevering and surviving through the tribulation. Let's look at the comparison:

You - 100 years King (Tops) + 1,000 years in Hell + when you do come out, you will forever be beneath me, a fitting future for a FOOL, and then just maybe if the balance is out, oh ohhh, and then into 'the Lake of Fire' you go, which even Demons Shudder at the Thought! (God's Words, God's Truth.)

Whereas on the Right-hand side, there is

Me - 100 years Low Life (in your eyes) + ∞ years Life, Health and Wealth as King + Co-ruler with Jesus.

Ironically, You still have a choice, which you never gave those children after you f#$%ed them, and then killed them, and then f#$%ed them again, and then as you served them to their parents, unbeknown to them, as a kind gesture in sympathy for their loss, you sat there Laughing inside as you Ate Their Child With Them!

You are an Abomination! Straight Into the F#$%ing Fire You Go! You Bypass Hell! No stopover for you!

Just Roast on that thought for a minute.
Tic tock, tic tock, tic tock . ., Tuck!
Your F#$%ed!

Rev. 19:20 states that the Beast and the False Prophet go straight into the Lake of fire; they bypass Hell. For it's a soul destroyer, you can't die, just Millions of years of intense pain until the Universal Cycle (Macroton) ends, and then it will spit them out the other side and MR HAWKING; they will REMEMBER. For my theory, the GOOD Theory Proves it. Whether you knew it, you f#$%er, you just gave them hope to keep doing Every Evil under the Sun, and for that, You Will Be Held Accountable, along with your F$%k Buddy, MR EINSTEIN, you decrepit Sons of Bitches. You and those f#$%en' CERN Demon Shiva Loving Bastards.

NO HOLDS BARRED, YOU C$*T. It's You Bastards who are releasing those Demons out on MASS. You Vicious Rotten pitiful existence for a Man! I was chastised amongst my peers back in 1989 for paying out on a bloke in a wheelchair with Motor Neurone Disease. I could see the pure Deception and Evil in your eyes back then but didn't even make a passing glance at your book, for my Spirit knew it was shit, yet amongst friends, I had to tolerate your dribble when one of your interviews appeared on TV. Yet by the early '90s, when a friend 'Enlightened Me' during a brief conversation and I saw your so-called great formula, that's when I knew that I was right all along. I come across your kind every time I walk into an institution.

You Malicious piece of sh*t, Repent or go to Hell. There, I showed you more forgiveness and respect than I do Most scientists. I just gave you a way out of Eternal Darkness, you wanker, which is more than what you have ever given in your lifetime, and just be grateful I didn't Vett you out sooner, which I should have.

Again, Repent or go to Hell. Five Words meaning ONE, Salvation. I'd take it if I were you. Your time is ticktocking away too . . . soon. (I wrote this before he died.)

To the novice, I become a much firmer, less relenting critic the higher up the accoladed ladder I go because they have influence over millions of lives. Briefly His (Hawking's) Theory was to prove(?) that no retention of memory or record within the Entire Universe will remain after a great contraction, which not only do I prove beyond a shadow of a doubt to be wrong but Also most importantly is opposite to what Jesus and God proclaim in the Bible. That's it in a nutshell, no larger than a spec!

Now you may be thinking, 'Why are you being so harsh? What's so bad about that?' I'll tell you. It opens the door for PSYCHOPATHS to not Heed God's STERN WARNING of Retribution after DEATH.

He's proclaiming One Life, No More, after Death Nothing; therefore, people on the verge of psychosis may tip believing that lie and carry out the most HEINOUS of crimes without any fear of payback. UNDERSTAND NOW why I'M SO ANGRY! He rates very bad, very, very bad in my books. He is partly responsible for the Rise of Apostacy and pointless living mentality amongst most troubled youth in the world today and inadvertently responsible for thousands of youth suicides throughout the world.

I'm actually holding out an Olive Branch, for I'm just not going to treat him with the same disregard he had treated the whole world. God expects me to pray for my enemies and offer salvation through Jesus to all. So then

'Lord God, may You Help Stephen and the rest of the apostate scientists of this world come to the realisation that you do exist and that the only way to eternal Life is to Repent of their Sins and to believe that Jesus is whom He says He is, Your Son, the Messiah and that the Only way to receive this Salvation offered by You is by making Jesus their Lord and follow no other. In the name of Jesus, I pray. Amen.'

(I feel better after that. Automatically, I felt a calm come over me; unfortunately, there's more chastising in need, for this very chapter is to deal with the Pharisees of today.)

Personally, I couldn't give a rats arse which way he goes; he's just another soul who backed the wrong side and gave up eternity for a trinket. I've got bigger, more influentially important Fish to Flip, of whose names you've probably never heard.

Logical Conclusion for the Existence of God

To the Atheist: 'You want proof of God?'
Then try this on for size (consider this), for here is Pure Logic from an Adept Mind.
I put this together round 2010.

- According to our observation of Physics, Everything in the Universe Is Unified.

- According to the Law of Symmetry, the Universe is Asymmetrical, where One overrides the other, i.e. there is an overall dominant Vector.

- Therefore according to this Law, it also implies that IF there is a State of Dimension, there MUST also exist a state of Non-Dimension.

- Therefore, this state of Non-Dimension supersedes Dimension (for Dimension is bound), and if consciousness exists in Dimension, so, too, it MUST exist within Non-Dimension.

Now according to the most widely reproduced book in the world, 'the Bible,' the Author claims that
- There is 1 and Only One God.
- God is both One and Infinite and.
- God is Outside Dimension.

This description perfectly fits our understanding of what the LAW just previously implied. On top of this is the fact that there is no other writing in the history of man that makes this ENTIRE claim!

One, Infinite and Outside Dimension!

Therefore, Logically, the existence of God cannot be Denied, and it would be in Everyone's best interest to find out what else this God of both the Bible and the Universe has to say!

So my advice to you, in all humility, is to get to know Jesus Now. Take it from me, For I would have to be one of (if not the) greatest amateur scientists that is virtually unknown in this world today. (I can say that because I've proven that.)

You must choose sides or be mopped up in the Greatest Onslaught in the History of Mankind.

For Satan's Army of Core dedicated Followers have already begun. The New World Order. This is their Solution, which is to create a state of constant War against Terrorism, and do you know who the terrorists are? You, me and just 93.33 percent of the World's Population. That's Who! Don't believe me. Then at least do you respect the American Journalist Walter Cronkite? Around 2003, he reported the growing trend of Civilians being slaughtered in wars since – Vietnam - 60%, Balkans - 70%, Iraq - 80%, Afghanistan - 90%. Do you get the Picture? Do you think this is the action of a Caring United World, or do you still think the World's Elite who Control Everything can't stop a bunch of Guerillas of whom they not only Fund but Also Sell Arms to?

Seriously, Wake the F#$k up. (If you're already aware, then please don't be offended by this repeated prompt.)

So as I'm about to begin to take you through the book of Daniel so that you, too, will be convinced as of who this MURDEROUS WHORE really is. Hitler and the entire fascist movement, Stalin and His Communists, England and her Pompous Imperialists and Hollywood and its Seductive Witchcraft Killing and Eating of Children don't come even close to that ABOMINATION that has lasted near 100 generations. I'm an Australian-born Serb, respectful for what my forefathers have SEARED deep in my Mind.

LEST WE FORGET!

Never again shall we allow our Children, our Heritage, our Loved Ones
To be Murdered or Slaughtered or Abused in any way!
Neither at the Front nor from the Rear, to the Left nor to the Right, from Above nor Below, in Our Schools nor in our Homes, via their Eyes nor through their Nose, through their Ears nor Mouths nor Senses from their Heads to their Toes.
For we shall rear them as the Good Lord Commanded.
In Christ Jesus, we'll Protect them and, in Faith, be well Founded.

Come, Lord Jesus, and Right this Wrong. Lead us in triumph against this unholy throng.
Anoint us for Battle with the Armour of God. Let us Advance forward throughout Gog and Magog.
Lead us with Wisdom Valour and Wit, from this Great South Land of the Holy Spirit!
As you've Proclaimed From Long ago, O Lord our God, Let it be so.

I Am No Man's Slave, for I was born Free,
For it's to God that I pray when I'm down on my Knees,
So I Choose to Live . . . and to Serve . . . . and to Die As I Please.

I repeat, 'I Am No Man's Slave. I Choose to Serve!'

So let's go back about halfway back when Daniel was just a lad.

Book of Daniel in Focus

The book opens with Nebuchadnezzar, king of the Babylonians, defeating the southern Israelite Kingdom of Judah at Jerusalem and takes King Jehoiakim of Judah and a group of the Nobility and high officials back to Babylon. Of them, Nebuchadnezzar orders his officials to pick out the most talented of Judean youth (of where the term 'Jewish' originated) to learn their ways and serve in his kingdom. Amongst these were Daniel, Hananiah, Mishael and Azariah. They were given Babylonian names – to Daniel - Belteshazzar, Hananiah - Shadrach, Mishael - Meshach and Azariah - Abednego. Now of them, Daniel was the most Talented and responded to the King's request to both know and interpret his dream without being told what was dreamt.

Daniel with his three companions prayed to God to reveal the information, and that night, Daniel received the vision of Nebuchadnezzar's dream and presented himself to the King the following morning. This was the vision which most of you would be familiar with. There was a large statue with

	Statue	Material	Kingdom	Divisions
1	Head	Gold	Babylon	1
2	Chest and Arms	Silver	Medea and Persia	2
3	Belly and Thighs	Bronze	Greece	4
4	Legs	Iron	Rome	2
5	Feet	Iron and Baked Clay	Rome Divided - (Babylon the Great)	2 - 10

6   The Rock, not cut out by Human Hands, strikes the feet, becomes a mountain, fills Earth and Endures Forever

Daniel's prophecy states chapter 2 verse 40 (Dan. 2:40) that the 4th is a final kingdom of the statue, yet the 4th is not only divided East and West by the legs but morphs to the addition of clay, 10 toes or 10 subkingdoms, links to Rev. 17 – 10 horns.
So the Statue is predominantly a 1:3 ratio of Nebuchadnezzar, the first and three that follow, this synchronises with the 1:3 ratio of Daniel and his 3 companions.
In verse 37, he states that Nebuchadnezzar is King of Kings and, in verse 38, Given by God.
This ties with Rev. 19:16, where Jesus is given the Name King of Kings and Lord of Lords.

So we see a cycle:
Babylon to Babylon the Great and
'King of Kings' to 'King of Kings and Lord of Lords'.

Now the 4th kingdom is different from the rest. Commentators recognise that when Rome moved its Capitol to Constantinople beginning the Byzantine Era, this depicted the division of the Legs similar to the Medes and Persians previously referring to the arms. However, there's a clear distinction between the feet and the legs where the toes of the feet are mixed with Baked Clay. Thus, our Ratio can also be interpreted as a 1:4. This duality is found Everywhere in the Bible as with Jacob/Israel or Abram/Abraham, which even though it is written clearly 4 kingdoms of the statue, we can see that the 4th can been interpreted as 2 kingdoms, which in this case, I numbered the Feet as a hidden 5th. This links to the Pentagram and Satan's Top Order and those who are named that WILL enter the Lake of Fire.

1 The Beast
2 The False Prophet in Rev. 19:20
3 Satan in Rev. 20:10
4 Death
5 Hades in Rev. 20:14

Here is the Counter 2:1:2 or 4:1 or 1:4 Ratio depending how you look at it.

Now when we compare the Empires to the Last Empire led by the Rock, Jesus, we see a 4:1 or 5:1 ratio. Where God's Kingdom is interpreted as Either the 5th or 6th kingdom.

As with time and the neighbouring relationships between the numbers 12 and 13 and 13 and 14, we can see transitional multi-neighbouring relationships amongst the numbers 3 and 4, 4 and 5 and 5 and 6.

(According to the Joke: Q. 'Why was 6 sad?' A. 'Cause 7, 8, 9!'

I conclude with Q. 'What gave Six Solace?' A. 'Nine attained Seventh Heaven with 11!' ;)

(For the Bible itself has many hidden relationships and meanings that require deep study to uncover the entirety of the message. These are like layers with a plurality of interpretations woven within the text. Let's consider the Bible text for a moment.

It's a book or Triality of
History, Law and Prophecy.
The Language is composed with symbols that are a Duality of
Words and Numbers,
1st and 2nd Testaments,
Hebrew and Greek or Jews and Gentiles.

Then the History talks of Cain and Abel, Ishmael and Isaac, Jacob and Esau, Sarah and Hagar, Leah and Rachel, the Kingdoms of Israel and Judah and the War between Good and Evil.

What we find are constant divisions, with History and Numerical patterns repeating as well.

Yet Also strangely enough, we find the Book Numbers, the Chapters and Verse numbers linking similar text with mathematical code.

Then we find the Amazing Heptatic Structure within the Text [groups of 7s] as discovered by Ivan Panin, which was most excellently described in Chuck Missler's '66/40' program and 'Learn the Bible in 24 hours' at www.khouse.com.

Also, the Geometrical and Holographic structures as found at the Bible Wheel and the Parallels between the Feasts and the development of the Human Foetus or the parallels between our Genes the Levitical breastplate and tribes of Israel and then of recent, the Equidistant Letter Sequencing [ELS] structure which again defies randomness or chance.

I'm sure you're starting to get the picture, But I digress; it's just too easy to do so. So back to basics and some nice simple bite-sized chunks at a time.)

What we also see is that we can tie this Statue with creation in Genesis where the Rock or 6th Kingdom ties with the 6th or final day of Creation when God said it was Very Good and rested on the 7th. Here's another 6:1 ratio highlighting the neighbouring relationship between 6 and 7.

Next point is in Daniel 3:24, where Shadrach, Meshach and Abednego were thrown into the Fire yet were not harmed. Daniel 3:25, 'I see four men walking around in the fire, unbound and unharmed and the fourth looks like a son of the Gods.'

Also Referring to One as Being the Son of God where Nebuchadnezzar errs and mentions Gods.

Again, Here's our 1:3 ratio as with Jesus and his three disciples – Peter, James and John – within his Inner Circle.

✿ The Writing on the Wall

We Continue now to the Central Part and Key Link to unlocking our Mystery 17, the Writing on the Wall.

King Belshazzar (Son/Grandson of Nebuchadnezzar) summons Daniel to answer the riddle, recognising that Daniel has Insight, Intelligence and Outstanding Wisdom in Dan. 5:14.

Daniel responds to the King and states that the King did not humble himself before God but rather opposed him and Praised Gods of Silver and Gold, Bronze and Iron, Wood and Stone, which do not See, Hear or Know (5:23).

In Daniel 5:25, he reads the inscription,

MENE

MENE

TEKEL

PARSIN *(NIV - UPHARSIN, KJV)*

Then Daniel interprets the inscription:

5:26 MENE: God has numbered the days of your reign and brought it to an end.

5:27 TEKEL: You have been weighed on the scales and found wanting.

5:28 PERES: Your kingdoms divided and given to the Medes and Persians.

In 5:23, Daniel mentions 6 false Gods with 3 inabilities. What immediately stands out is that the materials are the same as the previous dream by Nebuchadnezzar bar one, wood. What is interesting is that clay has vegetation or the root of wood amongst it. It's what gives clay the ability to absorb water and store it over longer periods than just sand and mineral alone.

So God to false Gods is a 1:6 ratio.

6 false Gods and 3 inabilities add to 9 with base 3.

(Also interesting to note that if we count God as 1, then 6 and 3, these are our triangular numbers in a broken order.)

Now 5:25 depicts a series of 12 Hebrew letters which adds to the chapter and verse number 5 + 2 + 5 = 12

and 12 sons of Jacob.

Now the numbers to chapter 5:25 are significant 5 squared = 25 a square, or 5 x 5 + 2 = 27 a cube, and

5 x 2 x 5 = 50 or the Jubilee year (signifying the stronghold Babylon held over the Jews was to be broken)

or 5 x 25 = 125, another cube, 5 x 2 + 5 = 15, the 5th Triangular Number and, finally, 5 x (2 + 5) = 35, which ties with the 3,500-year prophecy of the Return of Jesus.

Now we've pretty much done all we can with the two Prime functions, Addition and Multiplication. Again, we could continue with their reciprocals Subtraction and Division, but they are Secondary and belong to a different set.

So what we find amongst this group is 1 Square and 2 Cubes.

If we look at this Geometrically, as a solid cube consists of 6 faces, we can add the total number of Square Shapes, 1 + 6 + 6 = 13. Also, when we add the initial 12 letters with 13 Shapes = 25, our opening Square.

Keep this in mind.

Now verse 27 is centred between 26 and 28.

This is saying Square the Words with 27 in the middle.

This gives us 9 Hebrew letters numbered as such:

1	50	40
30	100	400
60	200	80

This totals to 961 or 31 squared and atbashed is 169 or 13 squared. Now only 12 and 13 can do this. They are mathematically very rare and what further links this pictogram to the Mystery.

Now the centre number 100 is 10 squared. This is the Primary Law, the 10 Commandments.

A Square within a Square, so when we Square the Opening Square, 25 x 25 = 625 or 6 + 2 + 5 = 13! Are you excited yet? Well, you bloody well should be, but now we'll sum it up with the *'Grand Finale'*.

The Square here in Daniel (the 27th book)

and the Triangle over in Revelation (the 27th book)

Again, the centre letter of the square equals 100 another Square! Here's a progression, a 9 numbered square to 10 squared. When we combine them, they add to 19, end of the Babylonian Cycle. Atbashed in Revelation 19 designates the End of 'Babylon the Great's' Cycle or Rule.

Are you impressed yet?

If not, I'm sorry for you that you come this far and still fail to recognise these very simple patterns that even certain morons could grasp. This did not happen by chance; it was orchestrated by a greater mind than yours and mine combined over millennia(!), and as Chuck Missler claimed and I reiterate,

'The Bible is an integrated message system from outside of our time domain.'

With all the power and weirdness the Latest 'D' Wave computers have, not even then could have mankind in total and one of those machines from day 1 have orchestrated or reciprocated in the least anything comparable to the Bible synchronising with the history of our species over the past 5,780 years to date (2020).

Mark my words. This is but a scratch compared to what others have found. Now if you're too lazy to research what others have already compiled or just don't have the time or patience, then just on the merit of what I've achieved and proven over the past 33 years, take it from me, there is no other book that comes within a whiff of the Bible. Oh, but there's more. Let's continue.

Now let's get a little more abstract.

Symbolically, another relationship between the Triangle and the Square is how one fits in the other. This highlights a Cross between Diagonals, which add to 200 and 181 when reading right to left beginning at the top.

If we subtract the latter from the former, we get 19. Also, when we add the top horizontal line, it adds to 91, and if we add the left vertical line, it adds to 91, another link to Rev. 19, only now also to the Cross of

KING OF KINGS

AND

LORD OF LORDS

The final Pictogram and its 191 Gematria.

Here is a merger of 19 and 91 no matter which way you read it, Right to Left as with the Hebrew Language or Left to Right as with the Greek. Jesus reveals 191 to both the Jew and the Gentile. Linking that to the subject Matter reveals at least 4 clear synchronicities between Daniel and Revelation in these particular verses alone.

Think about it. There are only 4 pictograms that I can recall – the 2 in Revelation, 1 here in Daniel and the Tetragramaton.

Yod, Heth, Waw, Heth in Exodus.

This is where it gets weird.

I did a study on Linguistics, where I'd found that by pronouncing all the clear vowel sounds we make, added to 9 distinctive sounds, the two semi-vowels 'Y' and 'W' would appear at opposite ends at the transition of opening and closing the mouth to make a continual sound between the vowels, 1 to 9 and back to 1. The uncanny thing is that whatever I chose to study would somehow link directly to this book in a more than profound way.

This is the Order:

Vowels:	u,	a,	e,	i,	o,	o1,	o2,	o3,	ir
Pronunciation:	up,	at,	et,	if,	of,	or,	good,	food,	bird
Semi-Vowels:		y	at	i			w	at	o3

Try it. Pronounce these Vowels in order and then repeat without breaks and the name of God, that so-called unpronounceable name according to some, rolls so easily off the tongue you'd think our mouths were designed for that very purpose!

Finally, 1 + 9 + 1 = 11 – the prophets' number

It's linked to the 2 prophets, Moses and Elijah, and Revelation Chapter 11.

> And chillingly to 11 September 2001 and the 911 US Emergency Call.
>
> Yes, those Demons planned it that way. I imagined a play. As they watched their plan unfold, their sick humour was to synchronise the Time and Date planned for this Deep State False Flag act of Treason. Realising the impending suffering they were to impose on the Americans, with glee, they cackled,
>
> 'Dial 911!'
>
> Their little inhouse joke, to the unsuspecting masses of whom they loath, showing nothing but utter contempt and hatred to their fellow citizens. Showing Absolutely No Empathy Whatsoever!

Remember this: Bush looks under his stand and remarks, 'No Weapons of Mass Destruction Here!' and the crowd erupts in laughter. This is the self-proclaimed Elitist's attitude to senseless Murder.

'Mindless Eaters' and 'Useless Breeders' are what many consider Christians and Truthers! Ohhh, their time has come, all right; the final 7 years has begun. Not a single one shall escape judgement.

Remember, Cain avenged 7 fold, Lamech 77 fold, Jesus 777 fold. Three times iterated will surely come to pass. That is The Law. Remember, if you sin against God or Jesus, you can be forgiven, but when you sin against the 3rd, Holy Spirit, there is no forgiveness; then you will wish you were never born!

Only an absolute MORON sells their soul for a trinket(!) or at all for that matter. My job is to wake up (Red Pill) the masses, the sheeple (as Bill Cooper termed those asleep at the wheel in the '90s) and at the other end of the spectrum try to Convert the Morons from self-annihilation and everyone else around them! No, I don't envy this task but knowing what I do.

'How could I not?'

Another interesting point is the 66 books of the Bible. When we go back to the biblical division of books I portrayed earlier, one division 6 x 11 books showed the Dynamic of SPIN in the shape and design of Ezekiel's Whirling Wheels (Cuboctahedral), where the fourth wheel acts on the horizontal linking the three pairs of 11 books together. Follow my posts at 'the Bible Wheel'.

NB Number 11 is also the 6th Prime Number, whereas 66 is also the 11th Triangular Number 11, which numeralises to 2 written as such 11/2 is known as the prophets' number. In Rev. 11, it speaks of the two prophets witnessing to the world. When we count 11 as 2 and multiply it by 6, we get, 2 x 6 = 12. Again, back to the previous Bible book order after Daniel appears 12 final Prophets that end the First Testament and usher the Second or the New Testament.

Indeed, the number 11 is strewn throughout the Bible and is generally connected to prophecy and a forewarning of a coming calamity, trial, war or tribulation upon a particular person, family, group, nation or, in this case, group of nations. From the first divisions in Genesis and complete balance in creation to the pillars before the temple and resting on the final two witnesses in the so-called 11th hour before judgement and complete restoration. Understanding how according to today's interpretation when discussing the modern-day concept of the doomsday clock, the time duration over the decades has shifted from the Eleventh Hour to 11:56 and is slowing down or everything else is speeding up depending on your viewpoint. What is interesting is how similar it is to the observance of Revelation. Basically, the closer we get to Zero Point or Ground Zero, the more accurate the forecast as well as the more corroborating evidence is found. Both are (according to time) travelling on the same rate of exponential increase, prior to the tipping point. It's an Epic Cycle similar to a Tidal Wave in nature, only with much greater force or impact upon our species, like an asteroid hitting the earth or getting blasted by a Z Class Coronal Mass Ejection from the Sun. Well, these Epic Cyclic instances are witnessed strewn throughout the constructs of the Universal Dynamic explained in the GOOD Theory.

What is also noticed is a certain strangeness to the Event which is Unique to its Mass. It could be seen as an optical illusion or seems to contradict natural law in some way, Anomalous somewhat Paradoxical similar to your time as compared with mine when one is observing the other fall into a Black Hole. The Faster Object 'A' travels in comparison with Object 'B' the Longer Object 'A' appears to Object 'B'. It optically seems to stretch.

Venn Diagram

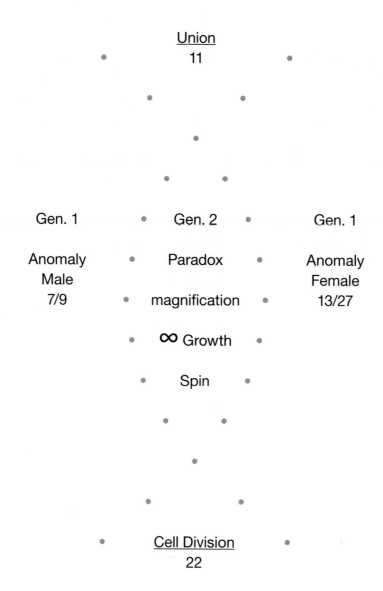

Union
11

Gen. 1   Gen. 2   Gen. 1

Anomaly   Paradox   Anomaly
Male   Female
7/9   magnification   13/27

∞ Growth

Spin

Cell Division
22

Where two Anomalous boundaries overlap, a region conducive to Paradoxical Behaviour is witnessed.

Before we continue, you may be thinking, what has this really got to do with prophecy? Well, Everything.

We can Already see Geometric Relationships with Prophecy and Matter; therefore, it makes sense to document these most fundamental aspects or combinations and build our Library of Numerical Meaning or Function for a better term. By showing you some of these basic examples will help you think about Numbers in a more Lateral yet more highly ordered and organic way than the current mainstream science you may be familiar with. This is Unified Theory, and I have to merge some of the Theory with the Biblical Links as we go along so that you can understand the meaning (Dynamic) behind the numerical Links and get up to speed with what I'm doing.

Now to get you well grounded, you'll need a GOOD foundation, and I just so happened to have stumbled across (over 33 years) the best in the world. It's a world's first visual multidimensional Theory of Everything called the Geometric Organisation of Dimension Theory or the GOOD Theory. I'll present it to you in two parts.

1. Pole Shift and the Nature of Spin
2. The Universal Cycle and the Origin of Spin

Pole Shift and the Nature of Spin

This One's for the Jews.

Many of you recognise the shape of the Merkabah or Stellated Octahedron. It's a symbol representing the Life Force, Vector Equilibrium *(Fuller: Cuboctahedron)* that's been recorded amongst some of the Mystical and Adept Teachings such as the Kabbalah. Well, I've discovered the Primary Physical Laws that manifest this Dynamic, which also just so happens to be the Missing Link in what Steers the Universe to Self-Regeneration!

What I'd discovered was that when a Tetrahedron is spun in space and initiated with one of its vertices at the pole, it pulsates, pointing one direction and then periodically turning to point 180 degrees in the opposite direction and back again. I've termed this the 'Pulse Effect' *(1992–2010)*, named after the Pulsar or Neutron Star. This effect is related to the Intermediate Axial Theorem *(circa 1830)*, the Dzhanibekov Effect *(1975–1985)* and the Spinning Tennis Racket Theory *(1989–1991)*. Now I've been able to prove that this Pole Shift is Equal to its Mass Density times its Spin or

$$P = ms$$ © Michael Banjanin 2010

You can view this action at my YouTube channel here:
https://www.youtube.com/watch?v=H4uKwvPez3c

Well, the Merkaba is what we see when viewing this action with a strobe light. The actual shape it makes is spherical, where two vertices will spiral North and the other two vertices spiral South, just like the 'Rodin Coil' (search Marco Rodin). This dynamic is like a hidden piece of <u>Newtonian Physics</u> that hasn't been identified until now, which I'm revealing to you. To cut a long story short, I've identified that this Dynamic filled in the crucial missing link to the 'Origin of Spin'. Yes, where energy comes from!

Well, the four-sided Tetrahedron *(the primary platonic solid, most tightest packed array of spheres)* –
the Tetragrammaton *(4 Letters)*,
the 4 Seraphim around God's throne,
the 4 Whirling Wheels each consisting of 4 interlocking wheels *(from the book of Ezekiel)*,
the 4 Angels holding Back the 4 Winds from the so-called 4 Corners of this Globe
    – are all geometrically related.

They're ALL related in God's 'Law of the Spheres' and every one of them Super Dynamic. The GOOD News is that we as children of God through faith in Jesus Christ can activate this Super Dynamism within us as well! But let's continue.

The Universal Cycle and the Origin of Spin

Now we can focus on the Main Frame of this Theory, for as I'd mentioned prior, we need a benchmark or a reference point as a basis. Our four Guidelines or Tools that we use to describe every aspect of existence are

<u>Language</u>　　　　<u>Mathematics</u>　　　　<u>Geometry</u>　　　　<u>Matter</u>

What we find is that once we put the basic rudiments in order, everything starts to automatically fall into place.

Our Mission is to now begin with the Primary Order and create our frame. We'll start with a Number Line.

<u>Math</u>:

e.g. We create a number line.

-9　-8　-7　-6　-5　-4　-3　-2　-1　0　1　2　3　4　5　6　7　8　9

Next, we draw a Dimensional Line and give it infinite parameters.

← -∞　-9　-8　-7　-6　-5　-4　-3　-2　-1　0　1　2　3　4　5　6　7　8　9　∞ →

And now we really give it some scope.

metres　←　-∞　10^{-50}　10^{-40}　10^{-30}　10^{-20}　10^{-10}　10^{0}　10^{10}　10^{20}　10^{30}　10^{40}　10^{50}　∞　→

x　　　　⇔　　　　X

This is a Decimal-Based Logarithmic Table. Now to get a handle of where you are on this scale, position yourself where the central arrow is between the two xs at 10^{0}, which is equal to One Metre in Length.

Now the smallest Subatomic Particle that we can detect is where Little 'x' is situated, at around 10^{-20} metres, which is a number 20 zeros smaller than you. Now the Largest Super Cluster of Galaxies that we can detect is where Biggy 'X' is situated, at around 10^{30} metres or 30 Zeros larger than you.

So now that I've condensed the our whole scope of the Universe, we can easily see between those two xs or about 50 Zeros in size. Also, for your sake, I've scaled down our scope of the Universe just so that you may perceive the scale ratio from our disclosed technological limits of 50 Zeros to what is commonly known as Googol 10^{100} or 100 Zeros.

Now if you like, feel free to visit my website at www.goodperiodictable.com, and if you click on the buy product tab, you'll get a good view of the front cover of the brochure we're selling, which depicts the universe as we know it on a logarithmic scale magnified X 2 as compared with this scale. You'll also notice that the entire illustration is held within the confines of a Toroid, which is the shape of the Magnetic Field of a Sphere. Now don't stay there for too long, for we will go back to that later. I only wanted you to see an Artistic Version of our Unified Table in its most Simplified Form so that I could hold true to my promise and show you a picture of what a Unified Theory of Everything can look like.

Now that you've had a glimpse, let's move on to solidifying this structure with rudiment Geometric Structure, for a picture without meaning, in this discipline, is a pointless exercise and an awful time waster of which I assure you I'm exerting to avoid.

Geo: Second Dimension - 2D - (Circumference)

For now, we shall take for granted that our First Dimensional (1D) Number Line or our String spanning a distance has an initial dynamic Spin force, and it begins to rotate around its midpoint like a propellor.

The shape it makes is a Circle - 2D.

Geo: Third Dimension - 3D - (Surface Area)

Now that the 1D - String is in full swing creating an artificial 2D Disc, the excess angular momentum is creating an overall spin on an axis spanning the Diameter like when spinning a coin on a table.

The shape it makes is a Sphere - 3D.

Now previously, when the String spun, the centre point remained Geocentric.

Then when the Disc spun, the centre point still remained Geocentric.

However, as this String material which is both Abnormally sparse in material yet very dense, so to speak, in energy (highly magnetic), we notice that the field strength is enough to propel itself through space in the direction of its South Pole. What we also notice is that the spin dynamic is causing a cascading effect of circular orbits within orbits perpendicular to the line of travel. Or like a series of Russian Doll concentric cork screw paths.

In fact, even before the sphere took shape, it was already moving away from its position. In relation to itself, it is spinning together, yet in relation to foreign bodies, it's displacement becomes apparent.

Let's table this.

				+ Spin
PD	or	Point Dimension	Px	
				+ Spin
1D	or	Line Dimension	x	
				+ Spin
2D	or	Plane Dimension	x, y	
				+ Spin

3D	or	Prism Dimension/	x, y, z	or the Prism becomes the Point
		Point Dimension		

Therefore, whether the particle PD covers all positions on its own like a Hydrogen Electron or connects with like particles like polymers to create strings or like a cell divides and grows forming string DNA which divide and grow, or just expand and contract or breathe in and breathe out like a Graviton, Quasar or Macroton does, or even Humans for that matter, then one thing is for sure, PD and 3D are similar; that is, in general, their major characteristic. That is, dimension to spin to mass density to life span to displacement and function are proportionally similar.

So the order goes 3, 1, 2, 3, 1, 2, 3 . . . etc. a Triality; Point/Prism ~ Line ~ Plane ~ Point/Prism ~ Line ~ Plane etc. or simplified as 3, 1, 3, 1, 3, 1, 3 . . . etc. a Duality: Point/Prism ~ Line ~ Point/Prism ~ Line ~ Point/Prism ~ Line etc.

Just Spheres and Strings. Now another way to picture our Infinite Universe is to observe One of these Spheres and look at its own individual reproductive (perpetuating) biocycle. Let's look at an Apple. When we take a Sphere of water and spin it in space, two things happen at once.

1. It curves in at the Poles and
2. forms a void on the inside.

This shape is similar to the Apple and its central Seed core. Now on a timeline, we can think of it as an Apple produces a Seed which transforms into a Tree, producing an Apple with a Seed becoming a Tree, etc. This is a Fractal or repetitive cycle, just like our Geometric Order of Spheres within Strings within Spheres within Strings, etc. Now provided the Environment doesn't change, these Apples will continue to reproduce forever. Now let's go back to the Good Periodic Table for a moment, where you will find that when I plot all the Atomic Isotopes according to Geometric Order, the shape it makes is a Torus, Magnetic Field or Apple! Where its major Tetrahedral division is in Five (5) parts. When you divide an Apple by cutting it along its Equator, you will notice it, too, divides into five parts. Back to the Atomic Table, as you read on, you'll see how the entire Apple Shaped Table fits within a larger table of Subatomic Particles, which is governed by the Same Tetrahedral Geometry within an Infinite or continuous cycle or Fractal.
Just Spheres and Strings. Hopefully by now, you've got a GOOD picture of how this Theory Looks and Relates to Basic Geometry so that now we can finally finish this section by explaining how all this information brought together can explain Where Spin comes from.

To summarise, when we add dynamic (Spin) to Dimension in space, a new cycle is created, one that is Perpetual (Fractal) and is Predominantly Divided into identifiable groups I've coined Plurality: Singularity (1), Duality (2), Triality (3), Quadrality (4) or even Higher Groups which involve internal Cell divisions or even more complex structures, beings or entities. So in light of this New Information or Pulse Effect (Pole Shift: P = ms), let's now consider how this may expand our understanding of the Universal Dynamic and see whether this Effect can explain any unanswered questions or Anomalies that we have observed regarding Macro Dynamics (Astronomical).

What we have observed is that in Galaxies, the most densest objects (e.g. Neutron Stars [Pulsars] and Black Holes) align themselves across the plane like a wiper blade or propellor to be more exact. Now physicists today believe that Pulsars are spinning on a wobbly axis like our Earth by trying to explain why we see peaks and troughs of X-rays that emanate from their Pole Regions. But as I've proven with the Pulse Effect, dense-packed objects that pack tetrahedrally change poles proportionally to their Spin, which both explains and predicts these observations to a 'T'. What we also have observed is that Quasars which are Galaxies condensed into a solar system-sized Black Hole (approximately 7 billion kilometres) have been known to line up in straight lines. Finally, the Hubble telescope's most distant vision of the Universe appears in a straight line!

Hmmm, there's some synchronicity going on here. Now when we bring magnets within an enough proximity of one another, they will align themselves so that their Poles are in a straight line.

No mistake, One Anomaly Solved. Yet let's continue. Some Universal models allude to a finite particle; others believe that the Universe stays pretty much the same. Yet I'm concluding that the Hubble vision is accurate and that our immediate Macrocosm I've coined 'the Macroton,' similar to the Graviton, does go through an Expansion (Big Bang) and Contraction (Big Crunch) just like Everything Else. Everything we have observed expands and contracts, everything is Fractal and Every individual or singular unit has its own Finite Cycle.

Now picture this: If you were to get a cup, half fill it with water, give it a stir and then float the cup in a larger tub of water, you'll notice that the cup will begin to rotate in the same direction as the water in the cup is spinning. So, too, with the Macroton, as many eddies are formed within, during its expansion process, an overall spin is created, which is due to the gravitational forces of the smaller particles within. Yet from the moment these individual Singularities begin to expand, the temperature begins to decrease, allowing larger particles to condense and coalesce. Now as the majority of the material begins to concentrate within these Quasars, the Vacuum or pressure outside in space will continue to increase to the point where it balances the gravitational pull of the Quasars, which is what is commonly described as reaching the <u>Tipping Point</u>. Now it is known that the uniform particles within these Quasars communicate throughout the entire Macroton instantaneously; in other words, they travel faster than light, which means the Expansion cycle would occur throughout the Macroton in a uniform manner, which is what the Hubble Telescope revealed. In other words, every Quasar within explode at exactly the same time. This is like a breathing process.

Therefore, as the Macroton breathes, this very action creates its own Spin.

Ahh, but hold on, what of the smaller particles, you may ask? Where is that Spin coming from? Well, let's size down and look at the Graviton. We conject that the graviton is a singular particle which therefore implies that it is similar to both the Quasar and the Macroton. If this is so, then as we see evidence of a Fractal Universe and Periodic repetition of particles over Dimension, we can conject that the Graviton would consist of even smaller Quasars (which I've termed 'Minars') being Fed by even smaller Gravitons I call Microtons.

Now this whole theory rests on One basis, which is that the Universe is both Infinitely Large and Small.

Hmm, Paradox. No matter which way we look, a paradox will be staring straight back at you.

A finite Universe: with no evidence or explanation for the origin of spin or

Just Accept the fact that the Universe IS Infinite with a workable model that not only explains the unexplained Anomalies that we can observe but also Boldly asserts how this Universe regenerates as well as where the Dynamic of Spin comes from.

To a lateral thinker, there is no Argument. Accept Infinity, where Everything Else adds up or believe in the Finite, and go right back to the Dark Ages of the twentieth-century non-deterministic chaos.

I side with Newton, and he sides with me; strangely enough, since Newton, few have added to the Newtonian Mechanical Model with an observable Law, of which range is equal to Gravity, as I have with the Pulse Effect. Where Not even One of the Quantum Cowboys of the early twentieth century have come close to what I have just revealed to you. For the Paradigm created by the Establishment post-Newton was totally biased against Bastardised Religion, which unfortunately steered good people away from God and His Infiniteness via Rebellion, Adopted Entropy, Destruction and a No-F#$%ing Certainty Principal which was orchestrated by none other than Satan himself.

Now I can speak boldly about this subject and even derogatorily towards certain scientists of the past, as well as the present, because I understand that a Man or Woman's flaws Will show up in their Theory. Whereas unless Pride and self-interest are put aside, and the seeker is willing to die to Self, can that person ever achieve what they set out to do. Well, I've been biding my time for the last 33 years, pretty much remaining silent and hidden from the spotlight, and why you may ask? Because of this Extreme biased control against Humanity and the TRUTH, where People Like Me are shunned by the Establishment because of the nature and law of Sin, for it will consume an entire nation or even species if Sin should be allowed to propagate. My kind of scientists have been silenced and killed off for millennia but not for much longer, for Disclosure and Transparency is increasing on a worldwide basis at an exponential rate, the fastest-growing paradigm shift movement today, i.e. who in the Western World is not familiar with the Matrix Trilogy of movies or hasn't heard of what being Red Pilled means?

Well, I had to be patient and wait upon when the Lord God enabled me to do so. I had to mature, for if I had of shot off any sooner, I would have been picked off like many others, and my efforts would have remained in absolute obscurity. *'Now is my time under the Sun'*, and my Enemies will not succeed against me, for I have foresight, and in seven years, our goal shall come to fruition. For I can now stand boldly and honestly proclaim that Nothing these Globalists attempt against me will succeed unless by the will of my Father and that only for the sake of honouring me through True Martyrdom. Not by blowing up a bunch of civilians at a public event or, even worse, by creating an Atomic Bomb or destructive devise like some. Hell no! Only by and through Faith in Christ Jesus do I die daily to live. That's why I have Nothing to fear, and I tell it how it is. I'm neither leaving my light under my bed, nor am I leaving this Planet in a hurry. That I can assure you. For God's Hairy Big Angels are protecting his own, and the wicked know it.

Unfortunately, the Pussy Christians who think they'll be raptured up will be in for a stark surprise, for I do believe this sh*t will really start to fly by 2023. Then only by an Amazing Faith shall they not capitulate and become Apostate.

Rev. 13:10 (NIV) states, 'This calls for patient endurance and faithfulness on the part of the saints', and again,

Rev. 14:12 states, 'This calls for patient endurance on the part of the saints who obey Gods commandments and remain faithful to Jesus' and 'Blessed are the dead who die in the Lord from now on' (14:13).

Twice reiterated only a chapter apart and then to finish with an extra blessing for keeping their faith to death from then on. Prior to 14:13 was already a blessing for those who die in Christ, yet an Extra blessing was decreed by God from that moment on because of how difficult it will be after that moment when the Last Trumpet will be fulfilled.

Make no mistake. Pre- and mid-tribulation Rapture is a deception from Satan, or do you still not understand what you just read? Then go to 1 Cor. 15:51, where not once but Twice Paul reiterates after the famous,

'In a twinkling of an eye,' event that the Dead will Rise **Before** the living take on immortality. This does not occur in Revelation until chapter 20, **After** the 7th seal, the 7th trumpet, the 7th final bowl of incense and the Final Great Battle *(or Armageddon, derived from Har Mageddon, meaning Hill of Megiddo)*.

Let's move on.

Some Prime Factors

I'll briefly touch on the Prime objective again by revealing these numbers:

Primes: 1, 3, 5, 11, 17 and 41 (Px)

1st 3rd 4th 6th 8th 14th

They all belong to the same group associated with these formulas:

$n^2 - n + 41 = 41$ Prime numbers in sequence, *Euler's Equation*

$n(n - 1) + (Px) = (Px)$ number of Prime numbers in sequence, *Banjanin's Equation*

Euler	Banjanin
$1 - 1 = 0$	$1 \times 0 = 0$
$4 - 2 = 2$	$2 \times 1 = 2$
$9 - 3 = 6$	$3 \times 2 = 6$
$16 - 4 = 12$	$4 \times 3 = 12$
$25 - 5 = 20$	$5 \times 4 = 20$

Can you see the difference? There are many ways to get to the same conclusion, but the road travelled is generally more important than the result.

Euler simplified the equation by squaring and then subtracting the number in question.

Whereas I was more interested in beginning with the number in question, which resulted in uncovering the same sequence of numbers, only phased back one. It's like when you fold your hands together Right by Left or Left by Right, you still get the same answer. My equation fully expresses the triangular pattern of the up and down triangles in Diagram 2 > Points of Interest > goodperiodictable.com.

See, with my equation, there is no bias between writing with your Left or Right Hand or writing from Left to Right or Right to Left.

Classic Atbash – what we should Expect to see. Oh, Euler's equation is a nice piece of work granted, but mine reveals true geometric order within the formula and guides the reader to understand the result in a whole new light – beautiful geometry, sheer poetry.

The best way I could explain the difference is your favourite fast food as compared with your grandmother's well-prepared, slow-cooked masterpiece. One is synthetic, the other natural; now you tell me, which is better?

The Counterfeit or the Original?

(No disrespect to Leonhard, for there's only so much one man can do or cover in a lifetime and without a calculator! Yet to this day, I still can't tell you which is harder, to create from scratch or to create the same thing with disinformation purposefully strewn throughout academia to the point that the instruction becomes more of a Red Herring than a help. An Impudent Impedance of the highest Degree, so to speak. However, amongst Scientists, he is one of very few of whom I will speak well of: Newton, Euler and Tesla – God-fearing men as far as I know. No doubt they had their faults as mine surely outweigh theirs, yet there is no way I will edify them above myself in any way. For we're all part of the same fraternity of Jesus Christ, son of the One and Only Living God creator of the Heavens and the Earth of whom is the source of

All GOOD inspiration. These men are my brothers of whom in hindsight, I will not refrain to criticise. This is my privilege, for we are of the same Calibre, and No, I'm not full of myself, for you can see with your own two eyes that my work speaks for itself. When you get to my level, then by all means, go scream your f#$%en' lungs out. It'll do you GOOD. We just need to tone it down a little. This is where very Mad, Angry men like myself need a balance and why I thank God I've got loved ones around me who can pacify my Anger and Frustration and criticise me when no one else can. Indeed, I am my own greatest critic and not because I'm just harder on myself than others but because my critique is constructive. Yes, I can be a persistently annoying f#$%ing cunt at times, disgusting, outright rude, disrespectful and deviant, yet even though I've possessed these traits in the past and know they are far from good, I will never state the contrary. In other words, I don't self-justify to legitimise my wrong actions; on the contrary, I explain what it is that made me so, as a warning, a correction, an understanding to others. Of course, I'm saying, 'Don't do as I do but do as I say.' So now you say that makes me a hypocrite? Go f#%k yourself! What would you rather that I just go ahead and rape your Arse like some Deviant Faggot Dog and say It's OK, this is natural, Normal behaviour and lobby in parliament to force 95 percent of the people to accept and swallow my shit (?!!!) and you say I'm Politically Incorrect? You Abominable Pieces of Sh*t! If you see yourself in this example and cannot see that I'm holding out an olive branch to you, then there is no hope for you. I do not try to legitimise or legalise my Sin. I recognise it for what it is. What You may call being a hypocrite is really an act of humility and righteousness to say to a minor. 'I'm not perfect. What I'm doing is not good.' Sure it's better to never smoke in front of my children, but I'm not there yet, and I'm not going to beat myself up over it because that's what Satan wants. Instead, I'm going to respectfully go outside and smoke away from them, but neither will I hide it, for that deception is even worse! I expect my friends to come out of their closets and just keep it indoors, OK. I don't shove my sh*t in their faces as they should Never shove their Mardi Gras F#%k Family Demonic shit in mine(!), and that goes double for Hallo-F#$%ing-ween. I don't go marching down the streets enforcing My Christian Values or singing Christmas Carols. Fair call? If you had any real Empathy in you, no matter what side you're on, you'd realise that what I am saying is Correct. You Know Jesus never forced anyone. He merely put a mirror up so that people could see themselves, and what they saw was so confrontingly disgusting that they either repented and changed their ways or got infuriated and tried to Kill Him!
That's the state of man, and it's getting to the point where everything needs to get sorted, which is exactly what is going to happen whether we like it.)

I hope now you can begin to grasp what I'm trying to express. Understanding prophecy is not a simple process. I had been fasting on and off for decades, yet it wasn't until I matured and lived like a prophet (all be it for only 190 days) before an anointing of understanding and revelation came upon me and in no small way.

Unfortunately, there are just too many half-hearted armchair critics claiming to be enlightened, who may live according to or even proclaim for a living, a particular scripture that appears once in the Bible yet will denounce another scripture or pattern that has been repeated many times. Chuck Missler warns us of this repeatedly at Khouse.com, straining the Gnat while overlooking the Frog, focusing on the Splinter while overlooking the Log! Need I say any more?

Back to the Prime Order.

To me, the linking of 41 to this group shows promise in a different study I'd done earlier regarding Jesus's Genealogy and the Mystery of the 3 missing Kings; 41 is also the total number of the Kings of Israel, Saul + David + Solomon = 3 + 19 Kings of Judah + 19 Kings of Israel = 41.

This particular study in itself is as epic as this exercise has been, if not more so.

I'll do what I can to rewrite these findings asap into a palatable piece of text that people can comprehend, and it will show some interesting patterns you may not be familiar with yet will be able to see that they are both real and revealing.

Recap

So now let's summarise over the key points or Synchronicities.

Nostradamus predicted that World War III and the Great Tribulation will have ended by the year 2027 at the latest, and the 1,000-year reign of peace *(age of Aquarius)* shall begin

Rev. 17:5 MYSTERY triangle tells the reader the following:
- There is something Jesus is revealing here, a hidden secret Mystery referring to the time(s) of when the destruction of Babylon the Great will take place.
- Gematria adds up to 8,857 = 521 *(99th prime number)* x 17

Bible scholars agree similarity exists between Genesis and Revelation.

In Gen. 17:1, God confirms his Promise to Abraham in his 99th year links to 521 *(99th prime Rev. 17)*.

Abraham is born in the year 1948 from Adam.

Isaiah's prophecy fulfilled, Jews return to Israel in the year 1948 from Jesus.

God first speaks to Abraham in his 75th year or the year 2023 from Adam.

2023 divided by 7 equals 289 or 17^2 *(Duration of the Final Week)*.

2023 + 3½-year tribulation period aligns with Nostradamus predicting the war is over by 2027.

Daniel's proven 69-week prophecy accurately predicts the Birth of Jesus.

The Final Week Duration depicting the Return of Jesus remains a Mystery to scholars.

Daniel prophecies about the times immediately preceding the return of Jesus.

Revelation predicts the same times.

The book of Daniel is the 27th book of the First Testament in Hebrew *(27 letter alphanumeric system)*.

The book of Revelation, 27th book of the Second Testament in Greek *(27 letter alphanumeric system)*.

The word 'Mystery' appears 22 times and only in the Second Testament, and the word 'Mysteries' appears 5 times and only in the Second Testament (according to the Strong's Concordance *KJV*). That's 22 + 5 = 27 times and always pertaining to the same message revealed in the Second Testament.

Daniel's pictogram Square (and Rectangle) plus Revelation's pictogram Triangle refer to numerical geometric function or to Square and Triangulate the code.

The number 17 is the clear key number in Revelation 17.
- MYSTERY triangle divides by 17
- Also reveals Global government of 7 heads and 10 horns adds to 17
- 7th and 8th head in Revelation link exactly to G7 to G8 global transition in the late 1980s
- Squaring 17 reveals one day 289 x 7 *(Daniel's final week)* equals 2023
- Mystery triangle appears in Rev. 17:5, 17 + 5 = 22 coincides with the times the word 'Mystery' appears in the Bible
- Psalm 22 also links to Jesus, which not only describes his crucifixion but of which the opening verse was quoted by Jesus as he hung there on the cross, 'My God, my God why have you forsaken me.'

(It astounded me to realise in His dying breath, He still taught us with Grace and infinite compassion under such excruciating pain. To His dying breath, He fulfilled what was expected of Him. Then came one of the most synchronous miracles of all, for as His blood ran down and touched the rocky ground, it caused an Earthquake and split the rock directly below him, to allow his blood to seep 6 meters through the crack to a hidden underground cavern, to land on a stone lid which cracked and moved apart to reveal and finally settle (sprinkle) on the Mercy Seat of the Ark of the Covenant! Hidden by Jeremiah during the Babylonian siege.
You couldn't make this stuff up. It's so beyond random and chance, so Bloody Perfect . . .
No, anyone who is that stupid, that ignorant, that proud to not recognise the superiority of whom Jesus really was and still is, anyone who dares trivialise what He did for us or compare Him with a prophet or, even worse, refuse in disgust, to mention his name . . .
To these people, what can I say but what awaits them All, well, it won't be nice to say the least!)
NB: Regarding the Finding of the Ark of the Covenant, search for Ron Wyatt's 6 January 1982 Discovery, 'Jeremiah's Grotto'.

From a different perspective, the Irish Catholic Pope Malachi predicted accurately 111 popes with synonymous figurative aspects regarding each pope in succession and then refers to Peter of Rome (Pope Francis) as the 112th and Last Pope before the return of Jesus. Ironically, the Irish use the term 'Malarkey' as pertaining to lies, which is the complete opposite from what we can see here with this very different Popes revelation.

Jesus Reveals Triangular numbers regarding the parable of the sower and the HARVEST.

Jesus tells his disciples in John 21:11 to count the fish being 153.
- 153 = 17th Triangular number = 9 x 17 = 9 numeralogicaly *(or 1 + 5 + 3)* Here, both divisors have a dual relationship with 153.
- John 21:11 numerically can be interpreted as 21 + 1 + 1 = 23 coincides with the year 2023.
- Verse 11 links this verse to a prophetic future event.
- 21:11 can simplify to 3:2, possibly implying a countdown 3,2,1. In respect to Rev. 17, it synchronises with chapters 17, 18 and 19, the final 3 chapters of tribulation in the book of Revelation.

- 17 + 18 + 19 = 54 = 2 x 27 the previous synchronous pair, Daniel + Revelation, Hebrew + Greek, Mystery + Mysteries.
- With paired synchronicities, 27, as the base number (does not divide by 2), is doubled twice, 27, 54, 108 – the Harmonic Nines. With Degrees, the reciprocal factors are 63, 36, 72 and 18.
- So when Jesus sent out the 72 (Luke 10:1), that number wasn't just picked out at random.
- T 36 = 666, 6(6 + 6) = 72, 6 + 6 + 6 = 18

'Now wait a minute,' some of you may be thinking. 'Aren't you just playing with numbers until you find what looks like a link. This is just random hocus-pocus. Why focus on the remainder!' In which by now you may have smugly convinced yourself so much that you don't even want to hear the answer. Well, here's One anyway to make you think outside your blocked mentality, and this one I picked up just the other day from another lateral thinker. Consider this:

For years, we've been taught that the earth's Axis is at a 23.4 degree tilt from the perpendicular point of the plane. So they added 90 and then subtracted 23.4 – classic Euler confusion!

The reference point is the plane. So when we add 66.6 degrees to the plane, we get the exact same position of the poles! Why add and subtract when we can just add? Don't be foolish and recognise that there are people in high places who don't want you to know or make sense out of anything.

Yet what they couldn't hide is that both 23.4 and 66.6 are part of the Harmonic 9 group as is with the note 'A' when tuned to 432 Hz as opposed to 438 or 440 when it was altered in the last century (for whatever diabolical reason). Now the earth's Harmonic 'Schumann Resonance' vibrates at 7.83 Hz, which just so happens to be of the Harmonic 9 group. 7 + 8 + 3 = 18, 1 + 8 = 9. This is how numerology works. You keep adding the numbers together until you reach a single-digit representation. It's a Difference Engine, similar to 'Babbages Calculator,' a Mathematical construct that Exists yet is vehemently denied as is the SO-Called 'Junk DNA' by the very same people who want to keep that information to themselves so that they may Monopolise and Control its Effect.

When it comes to distance, again out comes the chicanery! The reason we use multiple standards of measurement is so that when one shows harmonics amongst our celestial neighbours and the adept wish to hide it, all they have to do is switch from miles to kilometres or vice versa and, presto, no numerical significance!

Consider this, our planet Earth revolves around the Sun at an average speed of about 107,000 km/h or about 67,000 mph, yet just before and after the 21 June solstice (perihelion), that is around the first of May and the eleventh of August, the Earth will travel at Exactly 66,600 mph! This is no coincidence; this is the nature of Harmonics or Synchronous Cycles.

This wilful suppression of understanding far surpasses treason, for now it's leading to Worldwide Genocide (Agenda 21) under the lie that this planet cannot sustain us, backed by the same Demoniacs who control everything. Well, under these circumstances, how could anyone make any sense at all you ask? The answer is simple. God is Real, but you have to look and believe in what you cannot see. Life is predominantly a test of Faith. If you think all is lost, then consider this:

Isaiah 19:19 Pyramid Link

People wonder who it was that built the pyramids of Egypt, yet we now realise a vast complex of Megalithic structures that are found across the globe. Many think it was even extraterrestrial aliens responsible. Yet whoever built it is inconsequential to the point I'm about to make; however who designed it so is what really matters, for whomsoever was in control is surely working AGAINST the forces who are trying to suppress our knowledge in this world at the moment. You see the designer back then was aware of the two measurements we are using today — Imperial and Metric. Now this Designer realised that the changing of measurements would be one of the tactics of suppression humanities enemies would use against us in the future. So anticipating this, our very clever designer outsmarted them.

How? By using both measurements so that whether you measured in inches or centimetres, synchronicities would be found in the design using either measurement to prove beyond doubt who orchestrated it. Not all pyramids though. Only the great pyramid of Cheops does this. Much to the dismay of the Satanists, oooh, it infuriates them. For no matter how hard they tried, they just couldn't hide that big boy or the fact that it reveals itself in not only the mathematical languages of Yards and Metres but also according to the language of Geometry but most predominately in the most prolific read book in the world, the Holy Bible.

Read Isaiah 19:19. (I got this from Barry Smith in the early '90s.) In fact, to stop your slack arse from refraining to search, thus missing out, I'll quote it for you because I don't want you to miss this:

'In that day there will be an altar to the LORD, in the heart of Egypt and a monument to the LORD at its border. It will be a sign and witness to the LORD Almighty in the land of Egypt. When they cry out to the LORD because of their oppressors, he will send them a saviour and defender and he will rescue them.'

An Altar, a Monument, a Sign and a Witness – 4 descriptions, 4 sided structure (Square)
In the Heart, at its Border, in the Land – 3 reference points (Triangulated)
There is no mistake God is referring to the great pyramid with 7 distinctive points.
The Pyramid is actually an <u>Octahedral</u> complex, 'As above, so below' figuratively speaking.

It has 4 cardinal points – a top point, a bottom point undefined in the rock foundation below the lowest chamber and a Pyre Amid or Fire in the Middle. 4 surrounding and a pillar of 3 in the centre!

In the GOOD Book, you'll find God the Eternal light sitting on a throne, One with Holy Spirit and Son, a Triune or Three in one alignment, Up, Down and Middle.

Surrounding his throne are the 4 cherubim who have merged with the Whirling Wheels (<u>Cuboctahedrons</u>) from the book of Ezekiel, each one representative of Christ in the centre where the hot coals are that which permit one to speak prophecy (or the Word) and 12 Spheres or Disciples/Tribes of Israel surrounding him.

So if this Octahedron represents God, Jesus, Holy Spirit, and the 4 Seraphim surrounding the throne, 6 outer points + 1 inner point equating to 7, then what we find is that the description of the throne room in heaven in Revelation chapter 4 states that before the throne, there is a sea of glass. The Sea as in Rev. 17:15 represents the peoples of the earth. Now glass can be either Opaque, which can Reflect Light, or Transparent, which can Magnify Light. Above this Sea, also before God's Throne, Stands the 7 Lights or the 7 Angels.

Therefore, the 7 spirits are a Reflection of the 7 points of light in the centre. Now in this circle, we have the number 14, yet they are All above the Sea. Now if below the surface is representative of the Earth and Man's partially obscured, veiled or immature state, then as scripture proclaims, 'As above So below', we mirror the 14 above with 14 below, which adds to 28.

7, 14, 28 – our celestial timepieces. We have also now defined another relationship between the paired neighbours of 7 and 8 associated to the Octahedron.

Back to the Throne Room.
So if our First Sphere represents God, we could then table the order as such:

n = 1ˢᵗ Numerical Order		2nd NO	3rd NO	4th NO	5th NO	6th NO
Level	Entity(ies)	Progression	1st Diff.Eng	2nd Diff. Eng	3rd Diff. Eng	4th Diff. Eng
			+1			
1st Sphere +	God ⇒	1		+1		
			+2		+1	
2nd Sphere +	Jesus & Holy Spirit ⇒	3		+ 2		+ 0
			+4		+1	
3rd Sphere +	4 Seraphim ⇒	7		+ 3		**+13**
			+7		+14	
4th Sphere +	7 Spirits ⇒	14		**+17**		
			+24			
5th Sphere +	24 Elders ⇒	38				

(Recap on the Spherical Ratio's 7/9 (2D) and 13/27 (3D) in Root Geometric Order section)

Now as we can see by the table, the next groups that surround the 4ᵗʰ Sphere are the 24 Elders or the Fifth Sphere Links to our 5 Platonic Solids or our 5 exited states of the Sphere, which is a complete cycle. This links to the five divisions of an apple and the tetrahedral divisions or strings of the GOOD periodic table as well as the five kingdoms of Nebuchadnezzar's vision in the book of Daniel. The 24 are representative of the 12 Tribes of Israel and 12 Disciples of Jesus, which is corroborated in Rev. 22 when describing the names of the Gates in the New Jerusalem after only 12 Tribes, though technically, according to inheritance, there were 13. Also when describing the foundation levels named after the 12 Disciples, though, again, technically, there were 13. The parallels and synchronicities here become apparent when we merge the Language with the Mathematics and the Geometry. Letters, Numbers and Shapes – All are Symbolic.

Now this information is found in Rev. 4. Well, when we move Forward 13 chapters to the Mystery Triangle and chapter 17, we find the same 3 numbers linked in the order of heaven. In the 4th Numerical Order column in the 4th position, we find the difference of 17.

17 minus 4 remains 13.
1 + 3 = 4, they're related numerically.
1 + 7 = 8, which relates the 17 Mystery Triangle or Pyramid to the 8-sided Octahedral Double Pyramid with Triangular Faces, where Satan's counterpart are the Seventh and Eighth Heads of the Beast.

(For more information regarding the Great Pyramid, check out God's Great Pyramid *by David and Crystal Sereda, an amazing study and definitely worth acquiring. Visit www.DavidSereda.net.)*

There is no mistaking, God is whom He says He is, and what He says will surely happen, will most definitely happen. Sear these words in your mind. *(That means, 'Brand This in Your Brain!')*

'He is coming very soon.'

And these Global Elitist Satan Worshippers at the Peak of Free Masonry can't do a Goddamn thing to Stop it or avert what's coming their way. For us, it's freedom and a greater wealth than a Rothschild could ever imagine, and that's for the least of us, yet for them who fail to repent and rebuke Satan, well, they'll know what he's really like when they get to Hell. Deep down, he hates your guts, and the one thing he wants is to take as many of God's creation whom God Loves down to Hell so that he can torture the F#$%ers while he's sitting out his time, lamenting like a spoilt brat, like pulling the legs off the ants before the Trial and his ultimate fate.

INTO THE LAKE OF FIRE where the heat is so great it will burn his soul to nothing.

Until only his spirit is left and the Eternal memory and torment of the excruciating pain of having every sin he has caused burnt out of this existence, then he will be able to claim what it's like to feel just a touch of what God feels. Oh, but he won't boast after he goes through that he would prefer to lick the toes of God's lowest creature in front of everyone and everything so as not to remember the pain he will go through. He will regret for the rest of his existence that he abused his privileges. One minute in that fire and he will BEG Jesus to forgive him, but it will be too late. Every lousy part of him must burn and Vanish, for there is nothing within him that is written in the book of life. Death and Destruction he has Sown and will receive nothing less than Fire and Brimstone and an Infinite Agony of Agonies.

(To better acquaint yourself to these numerical patterns/relationships/anomalies, study the works of Nikola Tesla, Marko Rodin, Edward Leedskalnin, Walter Russell, Viktor Shauberger, Cymatics or Chladni waves, John Searl and his Law of Squares, Harmonics and Numerology.

And again, yes, NUMEROLOGY!

[To those who don't understand my emphasis, numerology has been shunned by the mathematical establishment, as Quackery has with Medicine, ever since its full potential became realised. Mind you, there are more home remedies and cures to cancer that the Quacks have discovered than what the World of Big Pharma would ever allow to be publicly disclosed!]

This is Adept or hidden knowledge that has been suppressed through the millennia. The corrupt have continued to infiltrate Every institution – political, religious or scholastic worldwide – to either Demonise these studies or Ridicule them. Indeed, mankind has always been at war over knowledge.

I have proven at the Subatomic Level that the Laws that govern the transition of matter from stable particles to unstable and back are directly linked to Numerology. I have done extensive research on this subject circa 1991 verifying this claim and can share this information with those who don't believe what I'm saying. [Another extensive study omitted for the sake of expediency of which I've yet to disclose to the general public, i.e. I printed a few copies and handed them out to those who've respected my work and were not going to argue with me till they're blue in the face from wasting my time trying to disprove what I Know and can Prove as Fact.])

Ezekiel's Whirling Wheels - Cuboctahedral Link

So now let's turn our observations to further conclude that as with Unified Theory, the Bible's structure and content show direct relationships with fundamental Geometric Law, just as I've expressed with the Periodic Table of the Elements, by just briefly touching again on where my scientific study synchronises with this study as I've extrapolated on my website (see: goodperiodictable.com) on the discovery that the Primary Geometric order (which is tetrahedral in nature and all based on the Primary Solid being the Sphere and the Spherical stacking Order, which is directly related to the Platonic Solid Order) is related to the relationships, physical dimensions and order of the Atomic Elements as well as ALL MATTER.

What I've also discovered and relayed at the Bible Wheel website back in 2010 and mentioned earlier is that Ezekiel's Whirling Wheels directly relate to the complete frame of the Cuboctahedron, which is formed when Stacking Spheres. Buckminster Fuller referred to this shape as the <u>Vector Equilibrium</u>.

<u>**NB**</u> The Vesica Piscis or, when multiplied, Flower of Life is Spherical Stacking or what I prefer to call the Law of Spheres as the Tree of Life, the Pyramids, Pre-Deluvian architecture and many artisan works of the world are ALL linked to the Sphere!

These symbols are synonymous or Synchronistically Linked with mystic and religious teaching throughout the world and all time.

What I'm revealing is this Link to ALL Science, ALL Matter ALL Existence in the One Theory I've termed the Geometric Organisation of Dimension Theory or the GOOD Theory.

It surpasses any other Unified Theory to date, from Einstein to Super Strings to E8.
Why? Because
it is One,
it is infinite,
it's Fractal in nature,
it leaves nothing out,
and it works!

Oh, and also since I first Published my work in 1997, no one in the world has been able to prove me wrong, debunk or surpass this Theory in any way, which I was and still am so gratefully privy to receive through my humility and faith in God.

Back to the Whirling Wheels, this Cuboctahedron is formed within when stacking tetrahedral framework to 4 levels. Now let's marvel at the Geometry; it consists of
6 Square faces,
8 Equilateral Triangular Faces,
12 Vertices,
24 Equidistant Edges, and
12 Spokes or 6 axial spokes,
which forms 4 interlocking Hexagonal wheels with 6 spokes each, where the plane of each wheel is angled to the 4 faces of the tetrahedron, and each spoke is shared by two wheels.

The description of Ezekiel's Wheels is obviously Linked to Geometry, in particular, the Mathematically Triangular Order revealed by Jesus and, in particular, the Mystery Triangle Rev. 17:5, the 4 Seraphim and the 4 horseman of the apocalypse and the 4 Angels holding back the four winds.

When you place Jesus in the centre Sphere, 12 other Spheres or Disciples surround the centre.

This is not coincidence; it is part of the Divine order and is found to be linked throughout every aspect of interpretation found in the Bible – History, Prophecy, Law, Parables and Teaching, Gematria and Code, both Figurative and Literal.

This Law of Spheres is RIDDLED (yes,dual meaning) throughout every aspect of the Bible and Life as we know it.

Conclusion

So what also became evident to me and to many others is that this Mathematical/Geometrical code is found in everyone's writing and forms of expression, even in our basic movements, and it's prophetic!

From casting Lots to reading coffee cups to speaking in unknown tongues, every expression can be interpreted!

This is 'Quantum Communication' (David Sereda) or related to of late what people refer to as the Law of Attraction.

For EVERYTHING is SYNCHRONOUS with EVERYTHING ELSE, and everything leaves a measurable fingerprint which can be interpreted

Mathematically,
Geometrically,
Literally,
Physically,
as well as Spiritually.

The revelation here is that it's everywhere and that the average person is oblivious to it!

Thus, the saying 'Can't see the forest for the Tree's' holds true in this case.

Well, not for very much longer, for this MYSTERY is now being revealed at an exponentially growing rate. It is also the nature of the worldwide Disclosure Movement and the end to the Demonic Deceptive Tyrannical Rule of the Globalist, Current Establishment or Cabal.

So 'the Mystery of Synchronicity' is that 'It Exists' and that everything is connected like Wheels and Cogs, Axils and Bearings, Springs and Washers, Nuts and Bolts, just Spheres and Strings!

This is the GOOD Theory and what the GOD does. It maps everything multidimensionally in geometric order.

Synchronicity Mystery (?) . . . . . Solved!

Mystery 17?

Well, you be the judge. I've just brought forward some very interesting synchronic links between biblical passages and prophecy regarding the coming expected Apocalypse. In conclusion, from all this compiled information, I conject that the 3½-year tribulation period will not begin at least until the year 2023.

The year 2020 will most probably usher in the prophesied false peace in the Middle East for the duration of half of the 7-year period or 3½ years. The double meaning between the year 2020 and the term 20/20 vision should inspire the timing of the Politically Staged Event or False Flag, purely designed to buy time for the preparation of the Great Conflict and the building of the Third Temple in Jerusalem.

According to authentically verified Astronomical findings, a smaller solar system associated with the term Planet X and one of its satellites Nibiru will definitely rendezvous with our system. Our Sun and the planet's average temperatures and tectonic displacements are still increasing, which means it's still coming in.

Cloaking such a large object from the people as it gets closer will prove to be challenging for those who are in power. I'm suspecting the arrival to be around the year 2025, coinciding with the wake of the next Solar maximum. The current position of this system can be detected through viewing the interference of the earth's magnetic cloud detected by our satellites throughout various times of the year.

Frankly, from what I can derive on the political front, the rise of Islamic agitation in the West definitely indicates a major worldwide problem, which, according to various statistical analysis, interpret that this will escalate to World War III and most probably begin by no later than the year 2030.

According to Jonathan Cahn's study, the Shemita 7-year Levitical cycle has preceded these major Events by a year or so, 1938 - WW2, 1966 - 7-day War Israel, 2001 - Iraq War, to name a few. With this in consideration, the next Shemita will fall in the year 2022, 1 year before 2023. Again hinting at the beginnings of conflict.

On the Return of Jesus and the final battle in the plains of Meggido (where the term Armageddon was derived),
these are the guesstamates:

Late 2026;	This Study, Nostradamus
2030 by the Latest;	Chuck Missler, Numerous Political Analysts
2048–2058	Jewish Prophecy (70 Jubilees or 3,500 years from the time of the Kings)
2240	6,000-year cycle (currently AD 2017 or 5777 Hebraic Calendar)

Again, you be the judge. One thing we all pretty much agree on is that these are
'Strange days indeed . . . . most peculiar mumma . . . whoa!'
Abomination, Apostasy, Anarchy, Androgyny And Atheism's Agenda is at the door of fruition, for thousands of years groomed for this moment. Standing in the doorway to progress. Impeding all who wish to pass through, including those who wish to come in.

'Behold, I stand at the door and knock. If anyone hears My voice and opens the door, I will come in to him and dine with him, and he with Me. To him who overcomes I will grant to sit with Me on My throne, as I also overcame and sat down with My Father on His throne' (*Rev. 3:20–21 [NIV]*).

Epilogue

Finally, I'd like to express the main purpose of why I chose to share this information. Well, it's not just for material gain, but I could do with some financial help, yet I've decided to keep it short, sweet and straight to the point, with the smaller condensed eight-page version (2017 edit) free online, but more importantly, if what I share can save a life and get people motivated to join the Worldwide Disclosure Movement headed by people like Stephen M Greer, Foster Gamble, Carl Munck, Ted Gunderson, Ron Paul, John Searl, John F Kennedy, Stephen Quayle, Julian Assange, Seth Rich, L A Marzulli, Walter Cronkite, Tom Horn, Kerry Cassidy, Chuck Missler, Fiona Barnett, Bill Ryan, David Sereda, Nassim Haramein, Tom Valone, Marshal Masters, David Wilcock, Kent Hovind, Linda Moulton Howe, Max Kieser, Dwight Eisenhauer and Granddaughter Laura, William Milton Cooper and Nikola Tesla (God bless their souls),Thomas Townsend Brown, Ed Dames, Richard E Bird, David Ike, Simon Parkes, John Pilger, Max Igan, Andy Pero (aka Superman, 'the Rhino': Montauk), Duncan Cameron (Al Bielic), Isaac Newton, Martin Luther, Philip K Dick, Otis Carr, Ralph Ring, Martin Luther King, Lucy Pringle, Richard Hoagland, Stanley Kubrik, Marko Rodin, Richard Dolen, Eric Von Danikan, Jacque Fresco, Eric P Dollard, John Hutchinson, Victor Shauberger, Walter Russell, Victor Grebenikov, Andrew Brietbart, Matt Drudge, Jesse Ventura, Alex Jones, David Knight, Owen Shroyer, Rob Dew and the rest of the Info Wars crew, Smith Wigglesworth, John the Baptist, Apostle Paul, my father Toma Banjanin (Clinton Killer) and cousin John (the Bomb) Banjanin who've spoken on behalf of those who've had no voice, Karen Hudes, Barry Smith, St Francis of Assisi, Richard Harrington, Edward Snowden, John Keely, coast to coast's Art Bell and George Noory, Donald J Trump, Wayne Glew, Tyler Glockner, Roger Stone, George Galloway, Joan of Arc, Stephen Yaxley Lennon (Tommy Robinson), Lauren Southern, Clifford Stone, Stan Deyo, Stefan Molyneux, Stan Meyer, Doug Hagman, Corey Goode, Mike Adams, Mark Dice, Nick Begic, Jim Mars, Robert Dean, Dr Slobodan M Draskovic, Quinn Michaels, Aaron Russo, Corey Feldman, Ted Nugent, Gary Allen, Robert O Young, the John Birch Society and 'Q', to name just a few and the Thousands of Fellow researchers and witnesses who have blazed the trail of exposing the truth for the Benefit of Mankind and especially the multitude who've paid the ultimate price in losing their lives for revealing the truth (we salute you and are ever indebted to the sacrifice you've made), then I can surely be rest assured that these efforts were not done in vain!

(Every time I'd read over this list, another name would pop into my head of whom I just couldn't leave out. There's just so many real trailblazers, but as far as light bearing and Revealing the Truth is concerned, of course, the Number 1 Position by Far goes to Our King of Kings and Lord of Lords **Jesus Christ**.)

For these are surely tumultuous times, and this whole world not only needs to get their heads out of the sands and wake up to what is going on but also need to be guided to a solution.

I figured during the stock market protests worldwide back round 2010, if the Group Anonymous had a political Platform with Representatives that people could have voted for, then all that exposure would have converted into votes and change of Government; their message would have made an impact.

Instead, their views and actions turned into no consequence.

So I've decided to create a New Political System and Platform called Constitutional Law Examination and Reform or the CLEAR Party, a place where we can make a difference through the power of the VOTE, a system designed to enforce Transparency and Invert the Power structure.

Very Simple and Effective. This is '*My Solution*', and here is my opening statement to the nations:

What is,
Constitutional
Law
Examination
And
Reform
or
the CLEAR Party
all about?

Introducing a new political system for the twenty-first century by Michael Banjanin.

Ever wonder why anyone would vote for or believe such an obvious liar? I mean, think about it, when you were younger, were you ever weirded out by these sleazy-eyed, repulsive and generally arrogant yes men, speaking a whole lot of jargon, making promises they rarely kept and somehow kept getting away with it?

Well, that's how I felt. It's also the reason why I exercised my right not to enrol to vote. I couldn't understand why a better system, a more honest and accountable political system, was never developed. As I got older, I got wiser. I recognised the system that satisfies the agenda of the Few who are in control, much to the detriment of society as a whole.

So I began to think about this. We are continually being conditioned to follow their propaganda, which is to keep us in debt, to be dumbed down and specialise in our mundane, mindless task-oriented job until we're either worn out or made redundant. We are, in fact, victims of a perpetuating parasitical system.

Think about this:

> If we are supposedly born equal, why don't we all have an equal share in our country as an inheritance?

> If this is a democracy, why aren't the people ever properly represented?

> Whoever made us believe the lie that the average human does not have the intellect to make simple decisions on laws based for the common good?

The answer to all these questions is based on lies and deception being fed to us by those who are currently profiteering on the backs of everyone else.

We are conditioned to believe that any real solution is only a pipe dream, a ridiculed Utopian Impossibility and that those in control do not Conspire. In fact, anyone who even hints at the Word Conspiracy is automatically ridiculed, earmarked as a terrorist or, even worse, assassinated.

Now you may say, 'Well, look at the past. They shot JFK, Martin Luther King all the way back to Jesus and beyond to the dawn of time. It stands to reason that we'll never change the Nature of the Beast that lives in us. For whoever we put in power, you know the saying, 'As power corrupts, ultimate power corrupts ultimately', eventually, they'll cave in and be like the rest. Am I not right?' You conclude.

Well, yes, you're right. In fact, it's the answer to the problem. ***Invert the power structure where 75 percent of members agree on the agenda***, where the minister is simply a signatory and spokesperson who has No Power to change what was voted. Brilliant!

Those who oppose could shoot our messenger, shoot our Kennedy, so to speak, and nothing would change, for we would have hundreds, thousands of Kennedys ready to fill that ministerial position. Shooting the minister or even the entire top-end brains trust would be pointless, for it could not force the will of the majority. This would automatically eradicate the ability for a minority or secret subversive group from taking control.

In other words, unless the majority were corrupt, no corrupted law or agenda could pass.

What I've been searching for is a fully Transparent governing system designed to keep governance, Totally accountable to the public for its actions and to eliminate corruption.

This is what prompted me to create the acronym of CLEAR – Constitutional Law Examination and Reform – a name which reflects that which is needed to be done.

The Aim is to unveil the truth, Full Disclosure to the public on all issues.

For I believe 'We Can Handle the Truth' and that the twenty-first century is ushering in a global ultimatum to our species,

> which is to either stick to the Status Quo and remain Slaves to an archaic evil system based on one of the most evil games ever invented on this Earth, aka Monopoly, or

> break Free from this tyrannical lunacy of dog-eat-dog mentality and finally grow up as the conscientious species we would like to be remembered for.
> A legacy worth fighting for
> For all our future generations.

Come, join Me and Billions of other like-minded people who have finally had ENOUGH!

Following are some of the main points I would like to see addressed, and if you feel as strongly as I do about any one of these goals, then I ask you in all humility to contact us and get involved. *For more information, go to clearparty.com.au.*

PS   Now after 32 years of abstaining to enrol, in this being my 50th Jubilee year of life on this planet, there is finally a Party Worth Enrolling to Vote For!
Even though I know I'm venturing out on a limb,
I'm still going for it!

Michael Banjanin
Founder of the CLEAR Party and
Husband, Father, Plumber, Scientist, a man of faith in God,
both sinner and saint, perfect I ain't,
just a fallible human being (2015).

Well, that was my Grand Opening Address to the World, and Remember,
it is One thing to discover a problem, it is another to Solve it!
What I'm offering is a REAL Solution,

For the Answer to Everyone's Problem is Clear, Very CLEAR!
clearparty.com.au . . . Get Involved and Evolve!

Thanks

Well, I hope I didn't Lose you along the way, but by no doubt, I'm sure you will agree with me on this one thing, which is that there's definitely a lot of cud for you to chew on here, for a while at least.

May God Bless Your Endeavours and bring revelation to the fullest. In the name of Jesus Christ, his son, I pray, amen.

Michael Banjanin
Michael@goodperiodictable.com
PO Box 980 Melton VIC 3337 Australia
+ 61 431 441 144

Notes and Anomalies

*[Note 1. *[1].] A few days later, I went back to get my blood test results, which came up well. The only thing was the doctor noticed my thyroid gland levels were out because of being low on iodine. I asked him of the side effects, which he replied that one can feel a bit irritated easily or short-tempered. 'No wonder', I said, 'why the prophets were such an angry lot!' The moment I got home, I swallowed two teaspoons of iodised (sea) salt and a glass of water and automatically felt that little more pacified. See, generally, I sweat more than most. Working as a plumber meant a lot of physical exertion. By the end of the day, my shirt would have dried caked on salt stains strewn throughout. By the evening, if I did not consume a copious amount of salt, my legs would cramp up excruciatingly. So much so my family members were concerned I'd hardened my arteries or harm my kidneys but not so. I drank a lot of water and avoided denying myself a drink when desired. Same thing with different foods. I learnt something from the chicken farmers, which when the hens could choose between three different pellets of varying nutrients, the eggs always came out better, and their overall health was remarkably better than the hens who had no choice. See, our bodies naturally know and crave the nutrients we need, which varies from person to person. The key is to not substitute the correct food with an ulterior substance. When you crave a beer, have a beer, not whiskey, yet when you crave an orange, grab an orange, and don't substitute or settle with a coke and chips. Your body knows. Listen to it! Now when it comes to junk, once a week or not at all. That's it. If you want to grow spiritually, fasting is a sure-fired fast track to self-discipline. Try it, one day a week generally won't kill you. Just do the right thing, stay in check and build it over time.*

Man, I knew of Pastors back in the 1990s going thirty to forty days, and they're still kicking today.

Now look at the contrast when the Irish hunger strikers did the same thing; they died as early as forty-one days. Why?

Frame of mind. Only recently, it was reported of an Indian Yogi living seventy days on air alone.

Discipline, moderation and gradual increments. But the number 1 key is Faith, and that doesn't come over night. So despair not, for it takes years for the most of us!

[Note 2. *2.] How Ironic is it that in 2017, when I wrote these very words, now in February 2020, as I'm about to publish this as a book for the first time, not only has the prophecy of the Temporary Peace Plan, recently negotiated by President Trump, occurred as I'd forecasted but the Term Spread Like a Virus regarding the Clear Party has also coincided with the spread of the Corona Virus. This time last year, we had around 150 members, by July, 200. After the Fed Election, I started to concentrate on the next election, pulled my finger out and grew to 400 members by the first of Jan. Three days later on the 4th, I set the launch date for this book. It's now Wednesday, 26 February, as this being the last item I write before this goes to print, and to date, we're over 600 members! Another coincidence?

I think by now you should already know the Answer to that question, but read on, and if you're like me by the time you get to the end of the book, you'll definitely read over these Notes and Anomalies again. That's generally when the penny drops, and it registers in your nut, the Second Time Around.

[Anomaly 1. *1.]

<(# Around May this year, a Strange Account, Wave or Anomaly occurred to me. What happened was that while I was putting this final edit together, I was revisiting the very same Nostradamus TV program to verify these dates, as you normally do before putting something to print. Well, ever since the first time I watched that program, I've always remembered the last date to be the year 3127. So you could imagine how to my astonishment while watching this same program again, thirty-eight years later, when I came to the part when John mentions Nostradamus's prediction for the end of this world, I hear a different year, 3797.

670 years further in the future!

It felt like I was in the twilight zone; really strange. I also felt conCERNed about the possibility that someone's been tampering with the past again, i.e. the Mandela Effect. It's a hot topic at the moment in the Esoteric World. Now normally, it would be a totally reasonable thing to assume that I obviously had it wrong from the start or just failed to remember this date correctly; I mean, it's been thirty-eight years, yeah?

Well, normally, yes. But when you consider
- that I was well interested in numerology by that time,
- that I was good at math,
- that my combined numerological number is 27/9, which I most definitely knew at that time and solidified the picture of 3127 in my mind since the 3 + 1 = 4 as well as the 2 + 7 = 9, and my Primary and Combined Numerological Numbers are equal to 4/9, then for a numbers person like me, it's

like you forgetting the name of your pet dog, if, say, your name was Rich and your dog's name was Bitch! You know what I mean (?). These numbers were significant to me
- that only ten years later in 1990, I'd noticed 127 as the 7th (end of cycle) number in the core sequence identified in my 1st Thesis, which was based on a numerological periodic pattern that I could relate to specific naturally occurring Isotopic characteristics (Subatomic Periodic Law),
- and that by the year 1994, I had memorised all the primes to 127, the 32nd number in the Prime 1 Group or the 31st(!) number in the Prime 2 group, then maybe I just could be recalling a rewritten past, which managed to still retain in my memory because of a series of highly significant and memorable reference points in time, directly related to that particular number.

So if there's anyone else who can recall this program as I do, be sure to send me an e-mail. I'd appreciate it.

Food for thought (You) and peace of mind (Me). #)>

[Anomaly 2. ⁎²·]

Here we go again. Ever heard of Andy Pero or Rhino boy aka Superman and the Montauk project? He's linked to the Philadelphia Experiment and the American Secretive Black Operations Group controlled by the Illuminati and the Free Masons of the world. Well, it seems my memory is playing funny buggers again. I read his account about seven years ago and just recently read through it again for the purpose of this exercise. Only I read a doctored copy (by Alan Branton), which I had stored. In the original text, he was interviewed by Eve Lorgen.

Well, in the original (about 100 pages long), he quoted a few things which were different from the one I have now. One item is that he was called Rhino Boy and not the Rhino, the other which I wanted to quote verbatim I couldn't even find, which is not an easy read. Because of his unwilling involvement with these diabolical maniacs who rule this world, his memory had been erased by no less than 1,000-plus times. But just like Duncan Cameron and many others (as well as Preston Nichols who himself was a Controller) who were involved at Montauk (Long Island, US), the memories began to reappear again of which they could verify. The account is patchy and repetitive, which makes the study much harder to fully grasp. Well, regarding the second account which was close to the end of his recollection and around the time he was introduced to the leadership of the Free Masonry (and was offered an honorary position amongst the 12 of which he refused), he made a strange statement of which a Bible Man like me would Never forget. (I'll paraphrase from memory.) He stated,

'The One thing that stood out amongst my conversation with these Beings was that they FEARED the name of JESUS. This caught my attention, I don't really understand why they would fear that name, but I thought I'd mention it all the same.'

Later, he mentioned that he was neither for nor against Christianity, for he wasn't brought up that way, which is why he found it strange. Whereas anything that could show a weakness to the Group that were responsible for torturing him throughout his life, he wanted to highlight because of his utmost hatred for these Mind-Controlling Psychopaths. We're talking about people or entities who, for whatever reason, swayed away from the adherence to God's GOOD Laws. Whereas the Bible explains that each generation that rejects Gods Law, this very action will cause their children to fall to the depravity of sexual deviancy and rule of self-will. This inevitably leads to a complete lack of EMPATHY for anyone or anything, a common phase to the decadent end of each previous empire.

Well, We are at WAR with Demons, and they will manipulate anyone they can. This is why it's so imperative

'to Train up your Children in the Ways of the Lord!'

We have a power that can contain these entities in Hell, which is <u>Empowered</u> by following in the footsteps of Jesus and BELIEVING that anything we ask God, in the name of Jesus, his Son, according to God's will, WILL Surely come to pass. 1 John 5:14–15 – Do yourself a favour and read all of 1 John while you're there; it will strengthen your Faith. You need it, and for that matter, so do we. We need Strong Allies, not Pussy Pew Warmers.

If you don't believe this, then you have already Lost,

(But this doesn't mean you can't come back. Yes, you were there in God's Bosom before the dawn of time. You were with Him at one stage in the past and can return at any moment, as can Satan for that matter, but we know he won't, for that <u>was</u> revealed to us, as for the rest of us, Kissinger, Bush, Rockefeller, (De) Rothschild, Clinton, Windsor, or Keating, for that matter, can all return at any moment should they choose. That's one of the things we the believers are not privy to know, which is designed to keep us on our toes!)

. . . for No Other name has this Power, not Michael, nor Mohammed, nor Krishna, nor Buddha, Brahma, Baphomet nor Satan for that matter. Here is a clear clue as to why the Good Lord made sure Andy's account got out. Because this is a War for the Future of Our Souls and God is in Control, therefore this is an individual TEST for all of us, which is another reason to FEAR GOD ONLY. Yes, He is the One who has allowed Us to go astray. You want to blame Him, by all means, Go Ahead. Yet in hindsight, you, too, will agree that it is better to have freedom of choice, that also includes the freedom to harm others, than to have no freedom at all! God Gave us the rules and only interferes when we Ask or when Satan does not play by the rules, which is pretty often. Now God said I will not allow more than what you can endure. I understand this because I know what it's like to be tortured but nowhere to the extent of what Andy Pero's been through. No pain, no gain? You better Freaking believe it. In fact, you know it. Andy's unique; as much as he hated it, he could take it, which elevated him to an indestructible level, yet there are billions who could not, of which God said, you've had enough, and they Died. Does this make sense to you?

I'm not condoning hurting self or others. Hell No! This IS how it is if you and I want free will. If God wanted us to be Robots, He could have made us that way, but no, we are living beings Learning How to Exercise our Freedom of choice. No matter how bad the environment gets, it won't stay that way forever; it's only until we have learnt our lesson. GOD IS IN CONTROL. Just remember, as a deterrent God said, that what we do against others at least the same portion will come straight back to us – 'An Eye for an Eye'. In other circumstances, a Double Portion is repaid for our evil deeds. This is Universal Law, a Balance with a Two-to-One Ratio (2:1). Two-part Angels to One-part Demons. In the End, the Universal Dynamic is headed towards GOOD, not EVIL. Yet it does go through it's cycle, i.e. from Yin to Yang. Here's your proof:

When the Universe is in the Expansion Stage, the majority of the elements are Hydrogen Atoms with a single Proton holding the majority of the mass, Two Up Quarks and One Down Quark. As the Universe heads towards Contraction, the majority of Elements that have not been compressed to singular Gravitons condense with a majority of Neutrons, One Up Quark and Two Down Quarks. Here is the 2:1 Ratio, which is Both Universal and Biblical. Let's now look at Cain. If anyone was to harm him, the repayment curse was 7 fold, Lamech 77 fold, Jesus 777 fold? (You be the Judge whether here is another mirror between the Genesis Law Breakers 1:2 ratio [Adam's 3 sons and Noah's 3 sons, where both Cain and Ham Transgressed the Law] and the Redeeming Revelator's 3 in 1 Tri Unity with his 2:1 ratio of Angels to Demons.)

Demons can control anyone if they are either unaware or wilfully allow it. This is why we need to pray for those who control our countries, for its Only through the Power of Prayer that can change them. This is our commission: 'To PROCLAIM the Good News of Jesus throughout the World and to PRAY FOR OUR ENEMIES. Yes, even people like Aleister Crowley or Adolf Hitler (if they're still alive, of course).

Our job is to Wake up and Win or Stay Asleep and Rot in Hell.

*[Anomaly 3. *³]*

<(# Regarding Pi, when you get the chance, you've just got to watch Carl Munck's The Code. He uncovers how the Atlantians used another way to express the Pi ratio, where 57.2957. . Degrees of the Arc or Circle is Equal to the Radius, where the Diameter equals 114.5915590261646. . Degrees. A Really Amazing Video.

I tend to prefer focusing on the Inverse Ratio: Diameter Divided by the Circumference 0.318309886183791.., and in particular, if Pi = 1, then the Radius Ratio would be half the Diameter Ratio or 0.159154943091895..

I find the Radius Ratio more repetitive and easier to remember. Also, it makes more sense to work on Dividing the Cell rather than multiplying a segment of the cell. Again, we see the Disinformationists at work, teaching all the students to first think of Pi in its opposite reality. For years, I couldn't understand why the Hell the world of Math used Pi upside down. Now thanks to Carl, the answer becomes Very CLEAR! Those Rotten Dirty Bastards didn't want anyone to understand Stonehenge, Giza, Nasca or anything! This goes beyond treason within a country, for its world-F#$%ing-wide! This is a deliberate covering over of the truth against HUMANITY!

When History is Deliberately Falsified and Heritage Hidden, there can ONLY be One Agenda, which is the annihilation of the General Public once they have been USURPED! That's Agenda 21, now Agenda 2030.

You F#$%ing Rotten Dirty Bastard Free Masonic Cunts are Finished! Your Game is Over.

Oh, and you better hope the CLEAR Party gets in control quickly; otherwise, there will be no Amnesty, and we won't be able to stop The Vigilantes from torturing you for years. Simply because Satan will get in their heads as he really hates you too. He's a Sadomasochist; he hates everything and everyone. So if you're with Satan, you're on a sinking ship. The sooner you jump, the better, and if it means he kills you for it, well, I'd rather be a no-name in Heaven than a King in Hell. You really think he's gonna help you? No Way. He's just like a Gay Slut. Once he's f#$%ed you, he doesn't want anything to do with you, you f#$%en' idiot. He's only interested in Vanillas, first-timers, virgins. You know why? Because he's pissed off with God, and he knows God Loves You. So when you get to hell, who else can you corrupt? No One. So then what good are you to him but be his little bitch lame dog that he can slap around for the next thousand years. For every time he looks at you, all he's going to see is his HATRED FOR GOD; now MARK, BRAND AND SEAR these 666 WORDS in your head and NEVER FORGET, for he Will unrelentlessly torture you day and night for the whole Thousand Years, for to him, that'll be like an all-night Bender, but for you . . .

Well, if you thought this life was long, then times it by THIRTEEN (13). Now that's a very long deep Samantha, Bewitched 'Weeeeell'. In the end, she could never justify her witchcraft family's selfishly evil actions, and the 'Well' strangely enough was prophetic! There is hope for anyone still alive. I just don't see many people leaving Sodom in a hurry . . .

. . . and I'm an Optimist! #)>

© Michael Banjanin 2020

Printed in the United States
By Bookmasters